Music Now

Music Now

A guide to recent developments and current
opportunities in music education

Dorothy Taylor

The Open University Press
Milton Keynes

The Open University Press
12 Cofferidge Close
Stony Stratford
Milton Keynes, MK11 1BY, England

First published 1979

Printed in Great Britain by
Billing & Sons Limited, Guildford, London and Worcester

British Library Cataloguing in Publication Data

Taylor, Dorothy
Music now.
1. Music – Instruction and study – Great Britain
I. Title
780'.72941   MT3.G7

ISBN 0 335 00253 6

Contents

List of diagrams and tables

Diagrams

Tables

Acknowledgements

An investigation of this nature has been made possible only through the co-operation and generous assistance of a number of agencies and individuals. To these, and to the many others who have generously contributed in some way, the author wishes to renew her thanks and sincere expressions of appreciation.

Particular thanks are due to Harry Armytage and Basil Deane who have been involved with this study from its inception. A debt is also owed to the many individuals who have generously assisted the writer: Edith Baer, Malcolm Barry, Patrick Forbes, Roger Harrison, Peter Haywood, Trevor Hold, Stan Kay, Alan Kimberley, James King, Alan Milton, Margaret Murray, Stan Roocroft and Geoffry Russell-Smith.

Grateful acknowledgement is made to the following sources for material reproduced in this book.

Figure 2   Hart, M. (1974), *Music*, London: Heineman Educational.
Tables 3 and 4   The Department of Education and Science (1975 and 1978 respectively). Reproduced by permission of the Controller of HMSO.

Foreword

This carefully researched book gives an excellent overall view of the phenomenal growth of the widespread activities of music in education.

It gives me great joy for I have always felt that music was an essential factor, an inescapable element, in the education of human beings.

The section entitled 'Landmarks in Music Education' makes fascinating reading and confirms that British musical life has become firmly entrenched in the traditions of these islands and nowhere does it flourish more strongly.

Yehudi Menuhin

A considerable debt of gratitude is owed to my husband and family for the tolerance and good grace which is always required in supporting efforts of this nature. Here the load has fallen on my husband who, throughout this project, has offered constant encouragement and practical help.

Dorothy Taylor

Introduction

Scenario: Friday 7 pm 197?

In a Nottinghamshire schoolroom a local brass band is beginning its final rehearsal for a national competition to be held next day.

Somewhere in South London a ten-year-old girl is having her weekly piano lesson at the home of a private music teacher.

A large group of first year pupils at a comprehensive school in Derbyshire has come back to school to rehearse for a forthcoming performance of *Joseph and the Amazing Technicolour Dreamcoat.*

Five Birmingham teenagers have secured their first 'gig' and are hard at work rehearsing their act for the all important date.

In Lancashire an audience of adults and children busily fill in a music quiz as they await the start of *Atarah's Family Fun Concert*, designed for maximum audience participation and involvement.

These are but a few examples of the vast number of people who, at any one time, are to be found participating in some form of musical activity. Whether it be in the home, school, church, club or concert hall, at whatever level, in whatever form, music learning is taking place.

In addition, these examples serve to show the essential interface between musical activity in the educational system and in the community. This is reinforced by, first, the pervading influence of music in everyday life (in the supermarket, home and car, through muzak, radio programmes and tape cassettes) and, second, by a dual system of examining music, i.e. the internal GCE and CSE examinations and the local external examinations of the Associated Board of the Royal Schools of Music and other leading conservatoires.

This book sets out to provide a synoptic view of recent developments and current opportunities in music education. It is a progress report and guide to a period of expansion when greater resources than ever before have become available to support the development of music education and musical activities generally. It is addressed to everyone interested in music education and its development: amateur and professional, adult, parent, student and teacher. In short, the book focuses on developments in the teaching and learning of music set against the background of major educational and societal trends. The writer hopes that the findings will be an encouragement to more informed discussion about the role, function and future development of music in education.

In general, according to common usage, the term 'music education' has been used to define music learning in its widest sense. This is contrasted with the term 'musical training' which connotes a precise activity such as instrumental learning or aural work forming part of music education.

The first two chapters set out to provide a contextual background for the period under review. Chapter 1 is concerned with historical determinants for music in education while chapter 2 describes certain post-war initiatives which appear to have had some bearing on present day developments. Chapter 3 identifies the increased range of musical resources and specialized provision which has become available in recent years.

Next, two chapters examine the music curriculum from primary to advanced level. More particularly, chapter 4 is concerned with the components of the curriculum from broad goals to instructional objectives, the effect of various influences on the curriculum, and finally music's emerging role in the school system. Chapter 5 describes the internal and external examination structures, the systems of advanced music education which they very largely underpin and the new avenues to learning opening up in adult and continuing education.

Finally, the last two chapters identify issues and opportunities which appear significant to the future progress of music education. An identification is made of particular areas of concern where greater professional commitment might do much to improve the value of music in education. This is followed by a summary of emerging opportunities which could provide greater accessibility to music and the arts.

It is the writer's hope that one of the strengths of this book is that it is not solely an account of a period of active and sustained growth. By the incorporation of a comprehensive appendix, the reader is provided with a guide to source material and resources which will help him to form his own conclusions about the contemporary musical scene. The material selected also serves as a basis for the reader's further development and general guidance in a rapidly evolving and very largely uncharted field.

Chapter 1

Historical perspectives

So free we seem, so fettered fast we are!

BROWNING, *Andreas del Sarto*

Early educational ideals

Throughout the history of western civilization music has played a perpetual, yet varying, role. In Ancient Greece music, as one of the nine 'muses', was integral to an educational scheme designed to prepare the freeman for a life of unlimited leisure. The young Athenian was taught to play the seven-stringed lyre and to make musical settings of lyric poems. He was expected to be both a composer and a performer. Anyone confessing to an inability to perform in this way was considered to be uneducated. An important reason for music's status in Ancient Greece was the fact that Pythagoras had discovered mathematical consistencies in tonal relationships. Plato is acknowledged to have been one of the first to stress music's intellectual values primarily on the basis of Pythagoras' findings (Hermann 1965, chapter 14).

Later the Romans emphasized the extrinsic value of music as an aid to the practice of oratory by encouraging melodious speech and controlled rhythmic gestures (Barclay 1959). By the time of Cicero (106–43 BC) music was recognized as one of seven 'liberal' arts. (Subjects known as 'liberal' were those originally regarded as branches of knowledge appropriate for freemen, contrasting with trades and skills practised for economic reasons by slaves or persons without political rights.) Within this curriculum music was considered so essential that it was one of the groups of subjects known as the 'quadrivium' – geometry, arithmetic, astronomy and music. The 'liberal' arts remained dominant in the university curriculum of early Christian Europe during which period a considerable body of music theory was developed.

The role of the Church

After the educational vacuum of the Middle Ages it became the function of the parish church to provide elementary instruction in reading, writing and music. The singing of plainsong was considered an art to be preserved and passed on to succeeding generations. Schools for church song were established by cathedrals and abbeys, the choir school of York Minster being founded as early as the year 627. An interesting account of a more recently founded church school, St. Michael's College, Tenbury, established in the mid-nineteenth century by Sir Frederick Ousley, is given by Alderson and Colles (1943, p. 72) who describe the place of music in the school's curriculum.

> The object of the college is to prepare a course of training, and to form a model for the Choral Service of the Church in these realms; and for the furtherance of this object, to receive, educate and train boys in such religious, musical and secular knowledge as shall be most conducive thereto.

Public school initiatives

The study of music in the eighteenth and early part of the nineteenth centuries does not appear to figure very prominently in the curriculum. There were notable exceptions however in some public schools. For example, at Uppingham School, Edward Thring (headmaster 1853–87) was notable for the importance he attached to music and art in his school's curriculum. Another public school, Hazlewood, was described in 1833 as a school which provided fencing, dancing and music, all taught by visiting teachers (Board of Education 1938). Although girls' high schools in the nineteenth century tended to model their curriculum on that of boys' public schools, in practice they usually placed less emphasis on the study of Latin and Greek and made more provision for the teaching of music, needlework and dancing.

Mass education

Nineteenth-century England witnessed the establishment of free education on a large scale. Before the introduction of state education with the Elementary Education Act of 1870 it was the function of 'charity' schools and Sunday schools to provide education for the underprivileged. Both types of school gave instruction in the three Rs and music was encouraged mainly as a means of improving hymn singing (see Winn 1954). Large concentrations of people had been brought together as a consequence of the Industrial Revolution. Living conditions were often grim and so church ministers tended to foster and encourage hymn singing as a healthy and alleviating activity.

The strength of this singing movement soon evoked an interest in methods of vocal instruction and music reading. Some account of the strong influence of the Church in the pottery towns, and of Methodism in particular is given by Nettel (1952, p. 4):

> Its nature made for the training of local leaders and singing was always regarded as one of its main virtues. But though hearty singing was an emphasised feature of Methodist Services, it was by no means confined to them; most denominations were anxious to improve the standard of congregational singing and from this common need arose innumerable experiments in methods of

teaching the art of singing and of reading music in some simplified manner which could be understood by a community containing only too often a large proportion of members either semi- or wholly illiterate.

Sight-singing teachers

Sight-singing soon became the backbone of nineteenth-century school and community music due to the talents of such teachers as John Hullah, Joseph Mainzer and John Curwen (Dobbs 1964). Methods of teaching music were already firmly established on the Continent, particularly in France where music teaching methods had been developed by Galin, Paris and Chevé (see Simpson 1976). John Hullah (1812–84) was commissioned by the Secretary of the Council's Committee on Education, Dr James Kay (later Sir James Kay-Shuttleworth) to study vocal instruction in the elementary schools of Paris and to prepare a manual for singing instruction suitable for use in English schools. The method which most impresseed Hullah and Kay was that of Wilhelm based on the 'fixed doh' system and, in 1841, Hullah's adaptation of Wilhelm's 'Method of Teaching Singing' was given official blessing by the Board of Education (Rainbow 1967).

In the same year Joseph Mainzer (1801–51) left France and settled in England. Within months he had succeeded in organizing singing classes similar to those he had held in Paris for working men. In quick succession he produced *The National Singing Circular* and a sight-singing textbook *Singing for the Million* which became the rallying cry for his campaign in London and the provinces as he made lecture tours and initiated nationwide classes.

1841 was also the year in which John Curwen, a Yorkshire Congregational minister, was commissioned at a Sunday School Conference to discover the most effective means of teaching young people to sight-read music. Impressed by the work of Sarah Glover, a Norwich schoolmistress, who in 1835 had published a scheme for teaching by sol-fa notation, he set about the task with extreme thoroughness. The first publication resulting from his efforts appeared in 1843 with the title *Singing for Schools and Congregations: a course of instruction in vocal music.*

The 'tonic sol-fa' system which Curwen ultimately devised was a carefully worked out synthesis of the 'movable doh' method of Sarah Glover and the use of her modulator chart, the time names (*langues de durées*) of Galin, Paris and Chevé, and the doctrine of the 'mental' effect of the degrees of the scale associated with another Frenchman, de Berneval. In the course of perfecting his method Curwen acknowledged not only his debt to the French musicians but also to other continental influences from Sweden, Belgium and Italy (Dobbs 1964, pp. 17–18).

The official seal of governmental approval which had been granted so early to Hullah's 'fixed doh' teaching method was to cause considerable friction between him and Curwen. Eventually, after practice had shown the superior worth of the 'movable doh' method, victory was finally conceded to Curwen's 'tonic sol-fa' system. Between 1853 and 1875 Curwen founded a publishing house, produced courses and manuals, established the Tonic Sol-Fa College and organized Tonic Sol-Fa Festivals at the Crystal Palace. His son, John Spencer Curwen, later took over the family firm, further sustaining the work of the movement through his own and his wife's active involvement in music education.

John Curwen regarded tonic sol-fa as an 'interpreting notation', a means to an end, and was quite explicit about this. In his *Standard Course of Tonic Sol-Fa* (1858) the means of gradual transferring to conventional staff note reading is fully explained. However, some of his most ardent followers lost sight of the real objectives of his teaching method and it was often taught as an end in itself. Despite this misuse his basic system has not only survived to the present day but has been regenerated through the work of Kodály.

Payment by results
It has been said that the British nation's fervour for sight-singing eventually became a mania (Scholes 1947). There are reports of annual gatherings in St Paul's Cathedral and at Crystal Palace. Here massed choirs, four thousand strong, from the London 'charity' schools, would sing metrical psalms, items such as Handel's 'Hallelujah Chorus' and Coronation anthems. These events were held regularly up to 1877. In view of this activity, it was very surprising to find that Forster's Education Act of 1870 made no reference at all to music as a school subject. This led to angry protests, deputations and even to questions in the House of Commons. Within a year or so, the omission was rectified and Singing was made a virtually compulsory subject in all Board schools. The Code of 1882 went even further by initiating a 'payment by results' scheme – sixpence per head for the rote learning of a specific number of songs, a shilling for singing by sight.

Between 1870 and 1900 music teaching in elementary schools was usually undertaken by the class teacher who had learnt the now fully systematized Tonic Sol-Fa method in training college. Yet by the end of the century, the craft of teaching sight-singing had begun to decline as teaching became less formal and the school curriculum wider in scope.

The prominence of the private teacher
With the decline of sight-singing a corresponding interest in instrumental music became apparent by the end of the nineteenth century. Ready availability of cheap, mass-produced pianos and violins created a demand for instrumental teachers (Scholes 1947, p. 726).

It would appear that to meet the new demand for instruction a new class of teacher had come into existence — one with no real qualifications and no professional standing and perhaps in most cases with some additional means of livelihood.

The sixpenny music lesson became a regular feature in advertisements where pianoforte and singing lessons were often offered in exchange for goods (provisions, drapery, furniture and bicycles etc.). Independent public schools with larger financial resources than state schools were often in a position to build up musical traditions which included instrumental tuition by visiting teachers. This tradition was particularly true of girls' public schools. At the same time home-based instrumental tuition became increasingly popular. This extra-curricular aspect of music tuition was possibly reinforced by the local (external) examination system initiated in 1876 by the Trinity College of Music and followed by the Royal Academy and Royal College which together formed the Associated Board of the Royal Schools of Music. By 1890 the Trinity College was operating over 100 local examination centres and the Associated Board 47.

Broadening outlook

At the beginning of the twentieth century, the educational philosophies of Froebel and Dewey were making an impact on the work of English schools. Froebel's interest in nurturing children much as a gardener tends a plant had a profound and lasting effect on the teaching of infants. Dewey's emphasis on the 'active' process of education and the relevance of the learning experience at each stage of development was drawn from his practical work in the school attached to the University of Chicago. The effect of these influences was seen in the gradual relaxation of more formal modes of teaching, the more active involvement of the children in the learning process and an increasing expansion of the curriculum.

Discovery

The influence of such men as Cecil Sharp (1859–1924) and Arnold Dolmetsch (1858–1940) on the music syllabus was strongly felt at this time. Although others had preceded Cecil Sharp in the collecting of folk song (including Lucy Broadwood, Frank Kidson and the Rev. S. Baring-Gould), it was Sharp who made both folk song and dance familiar to all sections of society. The use of the term 'folk song' was often misunderstood at this time and mistakenly applied to composed songs of the seventeenth and eighteenth centuries. When Sir Charles Stanford used the term inappropriately in the preface to his *National Song Book of 1906*, Sharp strongly reacted by conducting a fierce dialogue in the press with Stanford's spokesman Dr Arthur Somervell (then Chief Music Inspector) on the true definition of 'folk song' (Karpeles 1967, Chapter 6). To Sharp and his fellow collectors a folk song was music of anonymous origin chiselled and refined by many years of usage yet still, because of its innate quality, able to retain its original shape and characteristic features.

Cecil Sharp was convinced that the best means of making folk songs a part of everyday life was to ensure that they were learnt in school. To make this possible he produced *English Folk Songs for Schools* in 1906 in collaboration with S. Baring-Gould and many similar publications between 1908 and 1922 in the Novello School Songs Series. Sharp was recognized as one of the greatest educational influences of his time (see Karpeles 1967, chapter 14) and he played a prominent part in fostering folk song and dance in schools from 1905 until his death in 1924. During the last four years of his life he acted as an 'occasional' inspector of folk song and dance in training colleges, and his influence in discovering such an abundance of traditional musical material has been strongly evident up to the present generation of teachers and pupils.

Arnold Dolmetsch's specialization in early music and early instruments was first aroused by seeing a manuscript of seventeenth-century music for viols in the British Museum (Donington 1932). His revival of this early music led to an interest in the reconstruction of the instruments for which the music had been originally composed, i.e. viols, lutes, virginals and harpsichords. By 1919 his enthusiasm was concentrated on the reconstruction of the descant recorder. When completed in 1925 the recorder was introduced into schools (Scholes 1947). Almost simultaneously a parallel movement known as the 'Pipers Guild', which encouraged children to both make and play bamboo pipes, was initiated in schools by Miss Margaret James.

Dalcroze eurhythmics

Jacques Dalcroze (1865–1950) gave the first demonstration in London in 1912 of his method of music education through music and movement at the invitation of a London schoolmaster, Percy B. Ingham. As a young professor of Music in Geneva Dalcroze had realized that many music students were studying harmony without hearing what they were actually writing, due to insufficient development of the faculty of 'inner hearing'. By recognizing the fundamental place of motor–tactile faculties in the process of musical learning he began to develop his system of '*Gymnastique Rhythmique*' which became generally known as 'Eurhythmics' (Dalcroze 1921). The London School of Dalcroze Eurhythmics was founded in 1913 and similar schools soon appeared in Paris, Berlin, Stockholm, New York and other capitals.

In the belief that rhythm is the most powerful element in music, with a strong appeal to children, Dalcroze concluded that the most natural response to rhythm must be through a total muscular and nervous bodily reaction. He devised a series of graded exercises which encouraged pupils to react physically to musical rhythm (see Jacques Dalcroze 1921). In essence his training method relied on a year's basic training in rhythm followed by a course of *solfège* (pitch) in a rhythmic context, the study of harmony and finally, for advanced students or intending teachers, improvisation at the piano.

Dalcroze Eurhythmics were quickly assimilated into the timetable and the value of such training was constantly stressed by authoritative pronouncements such as the Cambridgeshire Report (1933, p. 24) which stated

> Rhythmic movements should find a regular place in the music scheme for some children find them the simplest approach to music and will obtain closer understanding of rhythm through bodily response to music. Boys who do this work with girls in the Infants' School and then drop it would also benefit by continuing such devices as stepping and beating to music.

and in a later section on Secondary Schools (p. 42)

> In some schools it is possible to arrange classes in Dalcroze Eurhythmics, which are very useful in the musical development of a pupil, especially if such development tends to be slow.

The appreciation movement

It was not until 1927 that the Board of Education's 'Suggestions for the Consideration of Teachers' substituted the subject title 'Music' for 'The Teaching of Singing' and it was about this time that the teaching of musical theory became noticeably less important. Instead more emphasis was placed on the need for the enjoyment and appreciation of music. Teachers came to believe that too little time was being allocated for teaching pupils to listen so that they might acquire intelligent listening habits for life. Significantly, in 1908 Stewart Macpherson (1865–1941), a professor at the Royal Academy of Music, founded the Music Teachers' Association, one of its chief aims being to promote the formation of musical appreciation classes.

In addition to producing important publications on aural training, Stewart Macpherson and his colleagues Ernest Read and Percy Scholes were the principal figures associated with the musical appreciation movement, which had originated in the USA a few years previously. Writing about first principles, Macpherson (1923, p. 4) states

> The main objective is to raise the general level of popular interest and understanding nearer to that of the artist: to show the plain man that a great art is worthy of his regard and – once that is admitted, to prove to him that such an art deserves a little trouble on his part to understand and appreciate it.

The dramatic change in attitude to the teaching of music seen in this period has been largely accredited to the work of Stewart Macpherson. An important landmark too was the birth of concerts and lecture recitals specifically designed for children which appeared as the natural outgrowth of the appreciation movement (see Charlton 1971). The first major concerts for children were organized in London by Gwynne Kimpton in 1911, and later by Robert Mayer and Ernest Read in 1923 and 1945, respectively.

The impact of gramophone and radio

For a time the growth of the appreciation movement was stultified until a revolution in mass communications provided the necessary impetus to make it a practical reality. After the First World War there were great improvements in recording quality such as the use of a microphone and the development of the electric reproducer. The gramophone record industry began to disseminate its products and in 1919 'His Master's Voice' company established an education department whose personnel assiduously travelled the country from end to end visiting classrooms, teachers' conferences, holiday courses and public libraries. Official recognition was given in the Board of Education's *Recent Developments in School Music* (1933) which pointed out that a school of any size could hardly be said to be properly equipped if it did not possess a gramophone and a good stock of records.

The classroom use of the gramophone had many detractors, as did the appreciation movement in general. It has been argued (see Moutrie 1968) that musical appreciation was made too easy for teacher and pupil and that the skills of the former were nullified and the latter relegated to an apparently passive role.

Commenting about the advantages and the disadvantages of the 'listening' aspect of music, in 1933 an official report (Cambridgeshire Report 1933) recommended that the balance of the music curriculum needed to be redressed on the side of practical work as against the less constructive art of listening.

Clearly the advent of both gramophone and radio must have had a dramatic effect on the general populace. Radio's beneficial influence was acknowledged early in the 1930s (Cambridgeshire Report 1933, p. 115)

> The effect of broadcast music on the general taste must also be mentioned: there can be little doubt that it is markedly raising musical standards, thanks to the enlightened policy of the British Broadcasting Corporation.

Schools (Educational) Broadcasting began in 1924 when Sir Walford Davies presented the first series of prototype music lessons for schools. Ten years later Ann Driver's equally famous 'music and movement' radio lessons made their debut. In many schools where there were no specialized music teaching available these lessons provided a valuable source of tuition and for the class music teacher offered supplementary ideas and stimulation.

The percussion band

Bramwell (1961) states that up to 1925 the playing of instruments formed no appreciable part of music making in the elementary school, although percussion instruments had been used to accompany a form of musical drill. Mention is made of the work of Miss Marie Salt who formed a percussion band as early as 1909. Her interesting work is described in an appendix to a Macpherson and Read publication (1912) entitled *Music and the Young Child — the Realization and Expression of Music through Movement.* Here Marie Salt explains her method of music education which she used at Streatham Hill High School with children aged four to eight. The use of percussion instruments, drums, tambourines, cymbals and triangles appears to anticipate by at least ten years the acknowledgement given to Miss Louie de Rusette for introducing the percussion band into schools. Again her description of free rhythmic movements interpreted in dance appeared to be closely related to elementary Dalcroze Eurhythmics, an educational method which, interestingly, was not demonstrated in England until 1912. Ernest Read's arrangements of well-known classical works for percussion bands in the 1920s led to the drawing up of a popular graded scheme of work for infant and junior schools. Work by Stephen Moore, Cyril Winn, Desmond MacMahon and Edmund Priestley in schools in Worcestershire and the West Riding of Yorkshire helped to promote and disseminate percussion band playing throughout the country.

Percussion bands were also encouraged and developed through the non-competitive festival movement as were violin, string and wind classes. This movement was founded by Ulric Brunner in 1927 and provided the opportunity for corporate music making free from the tensions of competition. Inevitably it provided a strong impetus to instrumental work in schools and particularly to the formation of school orchestras (Moore 1949).

The problem of 'group four': examination constraints

Although a vast expansion of musical activity had taken place in schools since the beginning of state education in 1870, music's status in the curriculum came to be severely handicapped by the system of external examinations introduced in 1917. The School Certificate and the matriculation requirements imposed by the universities and often demanded by employers were to exercise a profound and lasting effect on the secondary school curriculum. Music was one of the 'group four' subjects together with art, handicraft and domestic science. At first, although every one of these subjects was on the examination syllabus, a pass from this group could not be counted towards the final certificate. After much criticism the Board of Education eventually allowed group four subjects to be included but, as 'matriculation' status was still not granted, these subjects were widely considered to be peripheral extras. Not only did this prejudicial treatment affect music's place in the curriculum but it inevitably had repercussions on the quality of teaching by helping to filter out at the secondary school stage many potential entrants to the music teaching profession.

C. W. Valentine (1938, p. 26) discusses the dominance of matriculation requirements over school studies in these terms

> We must admit that the chief cause of the excessively academic nature of secondary school studies for many pupils has been the university matriculation requirements combined with the popular demand for 'Matriculation' even for pupils not *wishing* to enter a university.

He also comments that, at the time of writing only six per cent of secondary school pupils actually entered university. Why, he asked, should the curriculum for the majority be determined so largely by university requirements? The Spens Report (Board of Education 1938, p. 261) reflected growing pressure from associations such as the Head Mistresses Association asking for wider examination subject choice. The Committee representing the four secondary school associations and the Association of Education Committee made recommendations which included the total abolition of the 'group' system and the recognition of all subjects as being of equal value.

From 1938 there was a gradual relaxation and the eventual disappearance of the rigid group system, releasing music from its 'group four' strait-jacket. Although the School Certificate system was eventually superseded by the General Certificate of Education in 1951, in practical terms subject choice was still powerfully controlled by the individual requirements of universities. It was only when the alternative to the General Certificate Ordinary level, the Certificate of Secondary Education (CSE) was introduced in 1965 that a significantly liberalizing influence could be seen in the secondary school curriculum and in the music curriculum in particular.

Chapter 2
Post-war initiatives

When a man has obtained those things which are necessary to life,
there is another alternative than to obtain the superfluities: and that is
to adventure on life now.

THOREAU

A new spirit of exploration and co-operation affected all aspects of
society with the ending of the Second World War. This chapter attempts
to convey such feelings of post-war idealism by describing examples of
musical growth and experiment set against a rapidly changing social
scene.

Cultural democracy

A new concept of education and culture emerged in the years between
the two world wars. By the 1930s concerted efforts were being made to
make education, music and the arts more accessible to the general public.
Indeed, this inter-war period might be considered as the seed bed for the
'nationalization' or 'democratization' of culture which is now taking
place. The Rural Music Schools' Association, the Mechanics' Institutes
and the Workers' Educational Association were all pioneers in this mass
educational movement (see Minihan 1977) in company with numerous
music societies, associations and clubs which flourished at that time.

The effect of these endeavours, the influence of the BBC and the
morale raising powers of music and the arts which were evident during the
Second World War, led to the formation of the Council for the
Encouragement of Music and the Arts (CEMA). In 1946 CEMA was
renamed the Arts Council. More significant, however, was the actual
launching of such a project as CEMA during the war years, at a time
when so much financial and mental effort was being directed towards the
war effort. CEMA was established with a grant of £37,000 contributed
by the Pilgrim Trust. To this sum the Board of Education added one
pound for every pound until from February 1942 the Board was
providing sole support. The Council's lunchtime and midnight concerts
became regular features of factory life for workers on both day and night
shifts. CEMA also subsidized orchestras, operas and ballet performances.

In the first two years of its existence eight thousand concerts were
given, often in dangerous air-raid conditions. The Times, 26 February
1942, gave a full account of the musical situation at this time. The
Council's concern was often directed at specific groups such as evacuated
children, for whom series of lectures and concerts were organized.
Scholes (1947) and Moore (1949) both give accounts of the significant
part CEMA played in wartime. They spoke of its sustaining influence

and distractive value, pointing out that the general public was probably spending money on musical enjoyment as an available outlet when other activities and commodities were in short supply.

International co-operation

After the war moves were made to establish international collaboration in many fields including music and music education. For example, in 1953 the National Music Council of Great Britain was formed as a constituent member of the International Music Council which, in turn, was affiliated to UNESCO.

The first post-war international conference on music education, organized by the International Music Council, was held in Brussels in the same year. Attended by large numbers of music teachers, composers, performers and students, the aim of the conference was to determine the position of music teaching throughout the world and to discover ways of raising musical standards in regions where music education had not been fully developed.

Of the papers presented one, by Egon Kraus on the Orff–Bergese Method, introduced the first of several methodological approaches which subsequently was to have a significant influence on music teaching in British schools. Fresh impetus was also given to the revival of interest in folk music, the International Folk Music Council having been founded in 1947. In the introduction to his paper on the role of folk music in education, Sir Steuart Wilson observed that, paradoxically, some of the very agencies which had helped to destroy the traditional practice of folk music, such as primary education and the radio were now among those agencies contributing most effectively to its revival (UNESCO 1953).

Subsequent international conferences at Vienna (1958), Tokyo (1963) and Budapest (1964) were to acquaint a world-wide public with the work of Kodály and the Hungarian method of music education.

Opportunities for learning to play instruments

Perhaps the most important practical post-war musical development was the production of *plastic* recorders leading to today's situation where there are now more recorders sold, on a world scale, than all other instruments put together (Saunders 1978). Arnold Dolmetsch's early work, described in chapter 1, had by this time developed into a thriving family business. The leading exponent of the descant recorder was Arnold's son, Carl. He toured the country's schools giving recitals with the harpsichordist, Joseph Saxby. For many schoolchildren up and down the country these recitals were their only experience of professional concert-going. Here, too, were the beginnings of the 'Early Music' movement which is now rapidly gaining momentum in today's schools. The plastic recorder has many advantages – good tone, low manufacturing cost, virtual unbreakability and, most important, compactness and easy portability. Consequently local education authorities found these instruments relatively inexpensive and were able to purchase them in large quantities. At this time instrumental tuition was still rare for the majority of pupils either in the home or at school. Another reason for the success of the recorder as a classroom instrument was that, unlike the percussion band, the recorder could provide melodic interest.

Tests of ability
Gradually, however, progressive local education authorities began to introduce schemes providing free tuition on orchestral instruments for secondary school pupils. The founding of the National Youth Orchestras, that of Wales in 1945 and of Great Britain in 1947, reflected the growing desire to foster and organize instrumental music for the 13 to 19-year-old age range after the war years.

For economic reasons, tests of potential ability were used to choose those pupils who seemed most likely to benefit from such schemes. Psychological music testing was first associated with Carl Seashore in the USA (Seashore 1919) and the Measures of Musical Talent which he revised in 1939 were the first such tests to be fully standardized. In the United Kingdom, Herbert D. Wing was foremost in investigating the measurement, distribution and development of musical capacity (Wing 1948). The original purpose of the musical aptitude tests which Wing devised was to select musically endowed children who might benefit from musical tuition at the approximate age of transfer from primary schools to secondary schools. Whereas Seashore appeared to isolate the different components of the sound wave, i.e. pitch, loudness, timbre and time in a psycho-physical sense, Wing devised tests in which aptitude was measured always in a musical context. Thus the pitch of a note was not tested in isolation but by a succession of notes in a melodic line, simultaneously in a chord or, most commonly, in a melody with chords.

The work of Seashore and Wing was to lead to further research into the elusive nature of musical ability and the wide field of musical psychology by Arnold Bentley, Rosemary Shuter, Rupert Thackray and many others.

Music and secondary school expansion

The post-war rise in the birthrate reached its peak in 1947 with 881,000 births. It became clear that this expansion would lead to a 'bulge' of population in the 15 to 18 age group in about the early 1960s. The inevitable shortage of teachers was anticipated, however, by the provision of 16,000 extra teacher training places in 1958 and 1959, for already, with the publication of the Crowther Report (Ministry of Education 1959), the size of the bulge had reached over two million.

Before the 60s there had been no special emphasis placed on the particular stage of life between childhood and adulthood. Now the bulge had created a noticeable group of young people popularly known as 'teenagers'. Their world was one in which the economic transformation of the 50s had created more wealth and consequently more educational resources. Paradoxically, although greater family affluence reduced the need for children to leave school early, the attraction of earning high wages to spend on a swiftly expanding range of goods proved very tempting to the majority.

Despite the progress in music provision which has already been described, music and the arts did not always fare so well in comparison with other subjects in the timetable. For, as more and better qualified manpower was required in this era of technological advancement, governmental direction led to an emphasis on scientific and mathematical education. Recognizing the implications of this for the general balance of the secondary school curriculum, two government reports, the first on the 15 to 18-year-olds and the second on the young school leaver, repeatedly warned of the effect which such imbalance could have on subjects such as music and art. The Crowther Report (Ministry of Education 1959) found that, in general, girls' schools were attaching most importance to art, music and other subjects frequently labelled as non-academic. In many boys' grammar schools greater emphasis was being placed on gaining early 'O' level passes and on specialization for 'A' level and university entrance examinations. Understandably appreciably less time was being allocated in the timetable for the 'practical' subjects as they were termed. In The Crowther Report (paragraph 570) an argument was put forward for the scheduling of orchestral rehearsals within the timetable.

> ... that it is a task of importance to make this other tradition of artistic or creative education as much a respectable part of the general educational system as the largely analytical tradition of the schools.

Concern was also expressed about the use to which the young school leaver would put his educational experiences. It was suggested that the establishment of 'county colleges', for example, could provide opportunities for children who had played in school orchestras to continue this activity of 'amateur music making' as a leisure pursuit for life.

Four years later the Newsom Report (Central Advisory Council for Education 1963, paragraphs 268, 374, 413 and 418), concerned with the average child and those with less than average ability, made a survey of schools which showed that, in many instances, music was the 'Cinderella' of the curriculum.

> ... over half the schools have no provision for any kind of music.

> ... music offers distinctive experience of which too many older boys seem to be denied the opportunity, to judge from our survey.

... most of all, music is frequently the worst equipped and accommodated subject in the curriculum. It is only very recently that specific accommodation for music has begun to be included in the design of school buildings.

Attempting to redress the balance

Yet in the schools the contrasts are striking. On the one hand there are the individual schools or whole areas where music flourishes, extending beyond the classroom to choirs, orchestras, brass bands, concerts, informal club activities ...

As an appropriate example of such an oasis, the work of Peter Maxwell Davies at Cirencester Grammar School was widely acclaimed. His teaching there between 1959 and 1962 showed that unexpected achievements were possible when inspired teachers received support from sympathetic heads. Davies' compositional work for the school orchestra led him to encourage his pupils to produce their own original work including incidental music for the school's dramatic productions. Maxwell Davies (1963) has given an account of his pupils' experiences and compared them to children's painting in the art lesson, where creative work has had an acknowledged place for many years. It is interesting to note that, almost half a century earlier, musical composition was an integral part of the music lesson at the Perse School in Cambridge under the direction of H. Caldwell Cook. However, Maxwell Davies' work received even more publicity and emulation and is widely considered to be a landmark in music education.

The impact of the media

Developments in mass communication
Developments in mass communication proceeded rapidly after the end of the Second World War. The introduction of long playing records in 1949 soon led to the marketing of small 45 rpm records with a single song on each side. The popularity of this 'single' record was sustained by an increasingly affluent juvenile market which, in 1964, was reputed to be spending as much as £250,000 on 'pop' records every Saturday (Tucker 1966).

Technological sophistication had also reduced the wireless set to a transistorized unit. Lightweight, portable, it had the additional advantage of being small enough to be held up to the ear for sustained listening. Various 'pirate' radio stations sprang up in the 60s providing an endless stream of popular music for youthful consumption. In this way the commercial music machine, and, in particular, the record companies, were able to promote sales and maintain healthy profits. The BBC reacted by introducing a popular music channel, Radio One, devoted to day-long popular music.

17

Record, portable radio, tape recorder, cassette — technological developments were numerous and accelerative. But many people would consider television as the major innovation of the 1950s. Television was seen to take over the cinema's role as the prime medium for launching popular fashion. According to Swanwick (1968, chapter 4) the last fashion in popular culture communicated in the cinema was rock and roll in the 1956 film 'Rock Around the Clock'. Since that time records, radio, television, public performance and the press all assisted the spread of popularity of specific idols such as Elvis Presley, the Beatles, the Rolling Stones and Abba. The mass media demonstrated their capacity to be mutually reinforcing with apparent ease.

For many in the 1950s the television set became the dominating feature of the living room. In 1957 a new Saturday evening entertainment was introduced between children's viewing and adults' viewing time. Described as 'teen-time' (Whitcomb 1972) the 'Six-Five Special' solely featured pop music and was aimed specifically at the 15 to 19-year-old group. This was the prototype pop music programme. Higgins (1966, p. 22) referred to the way in which music could be exploited by such programmes to project a way of life, a new identity.

Most groups and singers try to sell an image rather than their music. This can be done much more easily on television where the viewers can actually see what the artist looks like, what he dresses like, how he moves on the stage or reacts to interviews.

Youth was not alone in proving a ready target for pleasurable indoctrination. Following American example, when commercial television began in 1955 music proved an ideal ingredient for promoting a product to the general public. Pastoral music soon became a musical cliché for cows grazing in the meadow, and, later, viewers were to be conditioned to anticipate a soothing relaxed feeling whenever Bach's 'Air on a G String' was played in the now classic cigar advertisement.

The potential influence and persuasive power of television aroused much anxiety, particularly in parents and teachers. Himmelweit, Oppenheim and Vince (1958) in their early survey on children's viewing habits, pointed out that every new medium of communication has, in its time, roused anxiety — 'the cinema, radio, and at one time, even reading!' Aware that children were being increasingly exposed to the influence of the mass media, the National Union of Teachers organized a conference in 1960 on 'Popular Culture and Personal Responsibilities'. Realizing that there were both advantages and disadvantages from children's exposure to television, one speaker reminded the delegates that the average child aged 8 to 16 was spending almost as much time with the mass media as he was at school. The main concern of this conference was that, in their opinion, television programmes tended to be over-weighted towards entertainment designed to please and distract. In the preamble to the BBC's charter, reference is made to the value of the broadcasting services as a 'means of disseminating information, education and entertainment'. Here is an implication that the three elements are equally important. On account of the viewing avidity of the majority of children, attention was brought to the obvious need for increased responsibility, discrimination and constant vigilance on the part of television authorities, parents and teachers alike to make sure that the 'entertainment' element did not cancel out the other vital two.

Schools broadcasting

Having briefly surveyed the impact of the media in general terms, what was the effect of the School Broadcasting Service on teachers, children and parents? In its early days, schools broadcasting had to struggle for acceptance as an educational resource. Regarded initially by many schools and teachers as an intrusion in the classroom there were also physical difficulties to overcome, such as poor quality reproduction and reception. Acknowledging the rapid pace of technology, Fawdry (1974, chapter 1) observes that today the situation is curiously one where the costly and elaborate installations which eventually solved these problems were to become 'white elephants', superseded by sensitive and easily carried transistor sets.

The early hostile attitude of the educational world was gradually overcome. Music programmes built up a large following in the early days of broadcasting, in particular 'Singing Together', one of the longest running school lessons, and Ann Driver's 'Music and Movement' series, briefly referred to in chapter one. In his preface to Gray and Percival (1962) Fiske describes how the battle for teaching young children good quality music and movement at the same time was won as a direct result of the BBC's broadcasts, initially inspired by the pioneer work of Ann Driver. Music and movement enthusiasts believed that it was essential to teach movement in association with *good* music so that young children could be given a pleasurable awareness of simple musical facts in association with movement and, by teaching them in combination, a greater saving of time could be gained.

A gradual tendency seen in education towards more informality in the teacher–pupil relationship was greatly assisted by the School Broadcasting Service. This was the view expressed by many school inspectors in the early 50s who stressed that a new situation had been created in the learning process, that of a more informal classroom atmosphere where pupils and teachers could experience the mutual joy of learning.

This experience was also extended to parents. An interesting side effect of schools broadcasting in general (Ministry of Education 1952) was that its influence was felt not only at school but also in the home. Evidence was found of housewives, particularly in Scotland, who tuned in regularly to the schools programmes, thereby becoming involved in a subliminal learning process. This serendipity factor was to end abruptly in 1973 when the schools service was transferred to a VHF channel which was more difficult to obtain.

Why should schools find broadcast lessons so useful? Hayter (1974, chapter 3) gives some reasons. First, that in certain specialist areas, particularly in music and mathematics, broadcasts are a direct help to the teacher who lacks particular specialist knowledge and skills. Second, that some teachers are concerned that broadcasts should be essentially concerned with the things which the teacher can *not* do; and third, some express their regard for the value of a new approach, voice or personality in the teaching of their subject.

The BBC (1966, p. 170) stressed the value of schools broadcasts as 'in-service' courses:

> The use of broadcasts in the classroom is also a significant factor in the in-service training of teachers when it involves them in new curricula and methods. The broadcasts not only introduce new methods but give the teacher confidence and continuity in using them, whether they be experiments in music on Carl Orff lines, modern mathematics etc.

An integral part of school broadcast lessons has always been the materials written to accompany them — the teachers' notes and pupils' pamphlets introduced as far back as 1925! In the early days of school broadcasting their value must have been inestimable, for it was reported that in 1939 only 68 per cent of the teaching staff were properly 'certificated' and that a quarter of these had never attended a college (Mee, 1974). Added to this were the adverse physical conditions of classes of 60 or more housed in old, decrepit buildings. It is interesting to learn that these pamphlets are as highly valued in the 1970s, for the number of schools buying the accompanying leaflets actually exceeds the number using the broadcasts (BBC, 1975).

By 1952 schools music programmes had expanded to seven series. 'Singing Together' and 'Music and Movement' were still the core programmes of the service. Television for schools was introduced in 1957 yet the first television music lesson did not appear until 1963, with the 'Making Music' series for older juniors.

But what could television specifically bring to music learning? John Hozier (1963) at the inauguration of the service expressed his view that television could follow the growing trend towards learning notation through the playing of instruments rather than through the voice as on radio. Not that radio was without its visual elements with its accompanying pamphlets showing melody and words, phrases with numbered bars, rhythm patterns and pictures of instruments. Television had new features to offer such as the electronic staff, which could perform the physical action for the child of moving the staff and illuminating the notes as he read. Instrumental work could also be prominently featured and note learning experienced through the use of fixed-pitch percussion instruments. In addition, playing technique could be demonstrated and a good teacher *shown*, in action as well as heard.

A new work commissioned from Richard Rodney Bennett, 'The Midnight Thief', appeared as the prototype for a number of works for television music programmes which provided opportunities for children to contribute their own improvisations as an integral part of the work.

A landmark series was launched in 1970, designed for the more challenging 13 to 15 age group. 'Making a Musical' was devised by John Hozier to actively engage the audience in creating a musical composition using a mixture of idioms such as 'pop', 'avant-garde', folk and traditional, and jazz. Using an approach developed by Sheffield's Theatre Vanguard incorporating extemporized stories, speech and drama, a musical play was worked out and presented by a cast of past and current pupils of a London comprehensive school, called the Mallory Opera Band. Also intended for this age group, BBC radio introduced a miscellany programme called 'Music Club' which encouraged audience participation while underplaying any formal teaching element. The increased popularity of the guitar as a school instrument was reflected in a new radio programme in 1972, 'Guitar School'.

However, in the same year the long established programme 'Singing Together' was already in its twenty-eighth year. To keep pace with the times new features had appeared. Guitar symbols were now printed for most of the songs. Melodic parts were demonstrated by orchestral instruments and the songs arranged for a variety of instrumental accompaniments such as chime bars, xylophones, recorders, drums and maracas. 'Music and Movement' was still very popular under its changed title 'Movement and Music' and used by 84 per cent of its target audience. The shift in emphasis from 'Music' to 'Movement' implied in the title could be attributed to the powerful influence Laban's work had on movement teaching in this country in the intervening years, which is discussed in chapter four.

By 1974 the seven music series had expanded to sixteen — fourteen on radio and two on television. The current vogue for participation, group work and informality is now reflected in such titles as: 'Music Club' (13 to 16 years, radio), 'Music Workshop' (8 to 13 years, radio) and 'A Corner for Music' (older infants, radio). As the title of the latter suggests, this programme is meant to be heard in the music corner and in groups of no more than five. Tape recording is considered essential so that, in time, the whole of the class can hear the programme. These programmes are counterbalanced by the more traditional 'Singing Together' (9 to 12 years, radio), 'Time and Tune' (7 to 8 years, radio) and 'Country Dancing' (8 to 11 years, radio). In addition to these, several schools broadcasts, including music, are provided by the local radio stations.

Independent Television has also made a significant contribution to Schools Music Programmes in recent years. One of the earliest, 'The

Magic of Music', was a mixture of story and direct teaching based on the principles of Kodály, aimed at the 6 to 7 age range, and first transmitted in 1972. 'Song and Story', an integrated programme of history and music for the 9 to 12-year-old, used traditional and contemporary songs of the period in a music hall setting in order to illuminate certain historical themes. 'Music Scene' for the 14 to 16-year-old group was aimed at a general audience of older pupils with a wide range of age and ability and not intended exclusively for use in music classes. Producer Christopher Jones (1975, p. 12) describes how this programme aimed to offer a framework of technical understanding to the average teenager enabling him to enjoy a wider spectrum of musical experience. Thus the musical components covered are melody, folk music, rhythm, African music, notation, harmony, tonality, analysis, instrumentation, modern music and music for film. At the same time he stresses the need for schools to use television as a resource not just for direct teaching lessons. The programme content allows scope for further work on simple topics of musical 'language' or for general discussion arising from the musical events shown.

As an educational resource, schools radio, television and, since 1964, radiovision have provided carefully structured, up-to-date materials at very little cost to those receiving them. As K. V. Bailey (1974) states in a short article on future developments

> In an era of scarcities (paper, postage facilities, packaging and transport) there are increased advantages in making material of excellence available by electronic means ...

Broadcasting is generally considered to have made a significant contribution to the practical development of many of the new ventures in primary education, especially in musical experience (Fawdry 1974). As it would appear realistic to presume that broadcasting will remain the cheapest form of large scale distribution of aural and visual material for many years to come, there is no reason to doubt the continuing value of its contribution in this specific area.

Chapter 3
Years of expansion

And thick and fast they came at last
And more, and more and more.

CARROLL, *Through the Looking Glass*

Advisers and inspectors

Increasingly in the post-war years local authorities appointed music advisers for the purpose of developing musical activities in schools. In addition, their brief was to cover staffing, accommodation, equipment and major awards; to organize instrumental tuition, concerts for schools, regional choirs, orchestras and festivals.

By 1959 almost half the authorities had appointed advisers (Long 1959) and by 1967 the figure had increased to 110 out of 135 authorities. Over and above this number and working in liaison with them was a number of music inspectors appointed by the Department of Education and Science. These inspectors (HMIs) were, as they still are, responsible for maintaining educational standards in schools, colleges and further education establishments, for running in-service courses and for acting as a co-ordinating body between the educational establishments and the national policy makers.

In recent years, following local government reorganization, certain changes have taken place with regard to the adviser's role and function. In some areas music advisers have been renamed general advisers responsible for the total educational welfare of a number of schools. Advising on music education (or on any other specialist subject) is now an additional responsibility rather than a primary duty. Viewed from one angle it is possible that advisers may be more personally involved in the general educational progress of a selected number of schools. An increased awareness of how music should function within the total scheme of subjects must be advantageous. On the other hand, it could be argued that the adviser's specialist skills may now be grossly under utilized, especially in a subject recognized as a teacher shortage area.

Instrumental schemes

With the increase in the number of advisers came the impetus to authorize peripatetic instrumental appointments and to inaugurate instrumental teaching schemes in schools. One local education authority, the former West Riding of Yorkshire had, by 1955, established both an instrumental scheme and a string quartet (The West Riding Quartet), part of the latter's function being to tour the authority's schools giving demonstration recitals. In 1961 the West Riding appointed full-time visiting guitar teachers and claimed to be the first authority to do so.

An account of the development of a city area scheme, in the City of Birmingham, is given by Adams (1968). In 1963 Stanley Adams was appointed as Birmingham's music adviser and 12 peripatetic teaching posts were immediately authorized. By 1968 the team numbered 24; violin and cello being taught in junior schools, woodwind and brass in secondary schools. Encouragement to hold supervised practices within the daily timetable was a means of testing if school heads and staff could regard instrumental work as an integral part of the timetable. Orchestras, bands and ensembles such as the Birmingham Schools Symphony, the Intermediate Junior String Orchestra and the Birmingham Schools Band were the natural outcome of a quickly expanding group teaching scheme.

Music centres

Hand in hand with the development of instrumental schemes has been the ever increasing growth of music centres. These can be divided into four general categories: centres maintained by the LEAs; Saturday morning music conservatoire schools; rural music school centres; and independent residential areas.

Centres maintained by the LEAs

These form the largest and most diversified of the four groups, approximately 200 in number (Gulbenkian 1978). Many of the centres which have been established since 1966 provide not only a base for peripatetic teaching staff but also cater for the needs of specially talented children. They often extend beyond the school age range to provide resources and training for the community as a whole.

One such centre is Salmon Pastures Music Centre in Sheffield, established in 1968. At the outset the Centre's accommodation consisted of one room in a junior school staffed by two assistant advisers and two part-time teaching staff. In 1969 the instrumental scheme was formally started in the Sheffield schools. Accommodation and staff increased until 1974 when the Centre moved into a disused school. By 1975 there were 36 full-time and 19 part-time staff teaching throughout the city area for four days of the week, with the fifth day spent at the Centre. At that time, 4,500 children received tuition in brass, woodwind and strings. The most recent venture has been to provide tuition in solo singing and piano, thereby venturing into an area which traditionally has been considered the domain of the private teacher based in her own home.

Apart from its function as the headquarters of the peripatetic instrumental service the many activities of the Sheffield Centre include: teachers' in-service music courses, bands, orchestras, guitar clubs, percussion classes, recorder consorts, aural and theory classes, 'O' and

'A' level courses, Saturday morning music school, teachers' orchestra and brass band, and the Hallam Sinfonia (the peripatetic teachers' own orchestra).

Dinnington Music Centre in South Yorkshire sprang up largely from the initiative of two headmasters. In 1969 they formed the Rother Valley Orchestra from forty adults, school leavers and schoolchildren. The orchestra soon expanded to sixty, meeting on Saturday evenings and giving occasional Sunday evening concerts. Premises and finance were initially provided by the College of Further Education until, in 1970, the West Riding Authority established the Centre on a formal basis and engaged sufficient part-time teachers to meet the demand for tuition in every section of the orchestra.

Although not strictly an LEA Centre, an extremely active music making centre flourishes in Liverpool. The Liverpool Youth Music Committee is a charitable organization, founded in 1956 to encourage voluntary music making among young people. Employing a full-time organizer to develop this work, a Youth Music Centre was established by 1970 and now has a membership of around 400 young people, of whom the average age is fifteen. The Centre functions on five days of the week and provides for all musical tastes. Its activities include ballet and guitar clubs, junior band and youth orchestra, jazz workshop, pop groups and choir and string ensembles (Mulholland 1976).

The tradition of music centres has long been established in technical colleges, for example Huddersfield's music centre was opened as early as 1947. The Ministry of Education's circular 323 'Liberal Education in Technical Colleges' (1957) has been described as a proven powerful educational force (Lowery 1963). The departments of liberal studies which were installed in technical colleges through the persuasions of this circular were to prove large spheres of influence not only for full-time students but also for the great numbers of part-time students who participate in evening and day-release courses. By 1963 there were technical colleges which had a concert hall, practice facilities, a symphony orchestra, choral and operatic societies, piano, singing and theory classes and could provide facilities for teachers' diplomas and music research degrees. A strong feature of music centres now firmly established in colleges such as Hitchin College, Southgate, Chiswick, Clarendon College and Huddersfield Polytechnic are the Young Musicians' Courses and the foundation music courses designed to prepare students for entry to university, polytechnic, music college or college of education. Usually consisting of two years' full-time study they are of great benefit to many sixth form pupils who lack full musical provision for 'O' and 'A' level examinations at school, either in instrumental or theoretical work. This type of education establishment also strongly appeals to those 16-year-olds who feel that they have outgrown their school environment and require a more mature atmosphere for further study.

Saturday morning conservatoire music schools

The Saturday morning music schools which form the core activity of a music centre's timetable have long been a feature of the music conservatoires. The Royal College of Music has run a Saturday morning Junior Department since 1926. Around the same time Yorke Trotter was organizing classes for children from LCC schools at the Royal Academy. His pupil, Gladys Puttick, is also known for her work both at Trinity College and the London College of Music where she has organized Saturday morning classes in the Junior Music School since 1960.

To become a Junior Exhibitioner at these schools prospective students must audition for places. If successful, many local authorities are prepared to make a contribution to the cost of the fees, sometimes paying the full cost. Often children travel many miles to attend these Saturday morning classes in the London Colleges. It is possible that the prestige attached to holding such exhibitions may be partially eroded by the greater availability of similar musical opportunities in the provincial and rural areas. Now that the Inner London Education Authority has its own music centre, the Centre for Young Musicians at Pimlico, it has ceased to assist places at the conservatoires, an example which may be quickly followed by other local authorities if the present economic climate persists.

Rural music school centres

Centres at focal points such as St. Austell in Cornwall and Trowbridge in Wiltshire are obvious assets in areas where musical resources might be otherwise widely dispersed. The Rural Music Schools' Association receives grants from foundations such as the Calouste Gulbenkian Foundation for the purpose of establishing and equipping new centres anywhere in the country. For example, to the Trowbridge Centre in Wiltshire, the Foundation gave £1,000 towards the purchase of a building and £1,200 for all the necessary equipment (Standing Conference for Amateur Music 1966). At present there are fourteen such centres in England where regular tuition and courses take place (Jacobs 1976, p. 169).

Independent residential centres

Dartington in Devon is an independent residential centre founded in 1925 by Leonard and Dorothy Elmhirst as an experiment in rural reconstruction and revitalization at a time when England was undergoing intense rural depopulation. For detailed descriptions of its founding and development see Dobbs (1975) and Bonham-Carter (1958). The Elmhirsts' orginal aim of making the 'arts' central to their concept of the reconstruction of the Dartington Estate has resulted in a complex of activities — a school, a college of arts developed from the former arts department, an international summer school and a Devon Centre for Further Education where short residential courses are held both for teachers and the general public.

Another example, the Rural Music Schools' Association, is a residential centre established in Hertfordshire. Founded in 1929 by Mary Ibberson (Ibberson 1977) it has been credited with pioneering work in methods of instrumental group teaching and has offshoot organizations such as the Association of Piano Group Teachers (established in 1962), the Association of String Class Teachers (1955) and the Wind Teachers (1965). Apart from its work in establishing other rural music centres it runs courses for peripatetic teachers from all areas on methods of instrumental teaching. The work of the Rural Music Schools Association has done much to popularize the Suzuki Method of Violin Playing, which has been the subject of a five-year research study (Rural Music Schools Association 1978).

Youth orchestras

In the preface to the Cambridgeshire Report on *Music and the Community* (1933) one reads:

> During the several years of preparation of the Report the Committee have observed with some apprehension the enormous increase in the *passive* participation of music which has been made possible by the gramophone and broadcasting. The value of these inventions as instruments of musical education cannot be denied but they carry with them the grave danger that we may become a nation of mere listeners that cannot sing or play an instrument.

Less than half a century later the compilers of this report would be astounded at the amount of musical activity being generated today. The accelerating growth of instrumental teaching schemes throughout the country is resulting in growing numbers of orchestras, bands and ensembles of every variety. The establishment of the National Orchestras of Wales and Great Britain has been briefly mentioned. Although thought to be the first *national* youth orchestras in the world (Redcliffe-Maud 1976) these were by no means novel ventures, for the first youth orchestras had been founded by Ernest Read way back in 1926 and 1931. Other national organizations to follow were: the National Youth Brass Band (1952); the British Youth Symphony (1956); and the National Youth Jazz Orchestra in 1965. One of the more recent additions is the National Association for Young String Players (Pro Corda, 1970) which gives progressive training in chamber music playing for young people. The fruits of this activity have been seen in the newly formed European Community Youth Orchestra (1977) where, after auditions, the United Kingdom players secured more places (44 in all) than any other competing country.

Yet the underpinning of these national and international ventures is certainly at local and regional level. Here such an orchestral explosion has occurred that it would be invidious to single out isolated examples.

Of the movement in general, however, there are several noteworthy features. Many areas have now built up a sufficiently large pool of players to be able to operate a three tier orchestral system in which children work their way through from school orchestra to elementary, junior and senior levels. It is fairly common for training to be extended and intensified through holiday and weekend courses. There is also an increasing trend for youth orchestras to make tours abroad giving public concerts and participating in international youth festivals. Indeed, today's mature performance standards are such that recording engagements are not uncommon while conductors and soloists of renown are drawn to offer their services, sometimes without fee, to some of the leading orchestras.

Instrumental schemes have gradually filtered down from secondary schools to younger age levels. Group violin teaching is one such activity which has become part of the timetable in various infant and primary schools, naturally dependent on the educational policy and financial resources of the different local authorities. This innovation has been attributed to the influence of the Suzuki Method, first demonstrated in this country in 1970, and made possible by the importation of cheap small-scale instruments (eighth, quarter, half-sized, etc.) from China, Czechoslovakia and Japan. It should be noted that violin classes for older children were also popular at the turn of the century when, similarly, a supply of modestly priced, mass produced instruments were available to add momentum to the project itself and, at the same time, create a demand for more classes.

The scope of instrumental teaching has steadily expanded to include as many instruments as resources of teaching manpower and finance will allow, e.g. harp, guitar and percussion in addition to the more usual wind, brass and strings. The National Schools' Brass Band Association, founded in 1952, has done much to release the brass band from its traditional all-male origins and to place it in a school context (Butterworth 1970). The Association's aim has been to raise the standard of repertoire as well as that of performance. This it is achieving by organizing composers' competitions, regional and national festivals and by commissioning works. So significant have been its achievements that, today, the once familiar musical comedy bandstand item has been replaced by commissioned works from composers such as Malcolm Arnold and Philip Lane, and by arrangements of works by composers such as Byrd, Gabrieli, Mozart and Grieg. In areas rich in brass band tradition parents prove to be particularly supportive both in finding the necessary funds to buy instruments and in being able to supervise home practice through their own instrumental expertise. Again, brass instrument teaching has filtered down to some primary schools where five and six-year-olds have been shown to make speedy progress in acquiring technical proficiency. The extent to which the primary school movement has spread can be measured by the fact that in 1975 the first brass band festival for primary schools was held at Sandwell, the programme including works heard twenty-one years earlier at the first *secondary* school festival.

On the other hand the wind band, concert or marching band is still a relative newcomer to British schools. American experience has shown that this type of band functions in two ways. It caters for the large number of wind players (particularly clarinettists) who cannot be accommodated in the school orchestra. This type of ensemble can also play a vital role in the school and community by performing at informal public functions and open air events. However, the number of wind bands has increased substantially during the last few years to a point where almost all secondary schools organize some type of wind group and are beginning to appreciate its potential value to the individual and to the school (Carlton 1978).

Courses

Holiday, weekend and summer courses for young people have become firmly established providing opportunities for young instrumentalists to enjoy intensive musical training with their peer group. In addition to the orchestral courses run by such organizations as the British Federation of Music Festivals and the Ernest Read Music Association, there have been recent developments of a more informal nature. Labelled 'workshops', they combine music study with outdoor pursuits such as swimming, squash, tennis and canoeing. The attraction of such a course draws not only the dedicated musician but also the musically interested and talented child for whom a continuous diet of music could prove too intensive.

Yet another interesting trend is the increasing number of courses for jazz players which can be largely attributed to the work of the Wavendon All-Music Plan (WAP) set up in 1970 by John Dankworth and Cleo Laine. This project aims to free music from the restraints of classification and offer as much diversity as possible. Thus music, according to the Wavendon philosophy, is capable of only two subdivisions 'good' or 'bad' be it classical, pop or jazz. The needs of musicians other than serious orchestral players were highlighted by Ashton (1975) when he stated that, of the 31,000 members of the Musicians' Union, less than 2,000 were employed to produce 'straight' music. As the remaining 29,000 were employed either full-time or part-time in some form of jazz or pop music making it was felt that major music institutions should equip themselves to provide relevant training facilities for these musicians.

Recently certain innovations have taken place to remedy this situation by bringing jazz and light music under the academic umbrella. The City of Leeds College of Music became the first institute in Europe to run a full-time jazz and light music diploma course. Goldsmiths' College runs jazz courses on a part-time basis and a diploma in light music is now being offered by the Newcastle College of Arts and Technology.

Vacation courses available to adults involved in music and music education abound in both the United Kingdom and abroad. In the United Kingdom alone, summer courses for July and August average around ninety, ranging from early music, choral classes, conducting and guitar at Canford to international saxophone congresses such as the one held recently at the Royal College of Music. Advanced courses are also available at the recently founded Britten-Pears School for Advanced Studies at the Aldeburgh Festival–Snape Maltings Foundation and at the International Musicians' Seminar at Prussia Cove near Penzance. Orff–Schulwerk summer courses are held annually in Salzburg's Orff Institute, and in Germany by Hohner, the musical instrument company. It is also possible to study the Hungarian Kodály Method in Esztergom, Hungary (see Taylor 1975).

Festivals

Ulric Brunner's non-competitive festival movement has steadily grown during the last fifty years or so to become the vehicle for displaying school and youth ensembles of all ages and forms. In many ways such festivals can be compared with the popular festivals of the nineteenth century which influenced choral standards, general musical taste and inspired composers to create new idioms of choral writing. The older type of competitive festival with its marks and positions still flourishes in many areas of the country providing opportunities for young and adult soloists, choirs and instrumental groups to measure their performance against others in a formal contest atmosphere. The Welsh Eisteddfod is an obvious example. Yet it is the non-competitive festival movement which, particularly over the last decade, has continued to grow, attracting considerable support and ever increasing publicity.

The most prominent and prestigious youth music festival however is a successful compromise between competition and non-competition, where there are no winners or losers but awards and commendations presented by individual sponsors at the discretion of the adjudicators.

The first National Festival of Music for Youth was launched in 1971 with events taking place over a two-day period. The finalists were selected from tape recordings sent in by numerous orchestras, bands, recorder groups etc. By 1974 a marking system had been dropped in favour of 'live' heats on a regional basis. Adjudicators selected the most outstanding performers to participate in what now became a three-day festival at Fairfields Hall, Croydon. The standard of performance here was so high that twelve ensembles were chosen to appear at the first School Prom at the Royal Albert Hall. The diversity of ensembles can be seen from the programme – concert band, chamber ensembles, steel band, orchestras, dance band and big band, wind quintet, oboe quartet, recorder consort, and accordion orchestra. Music correspondent Robin Maconie (1975b) commented on the developments which had taken place during the first four years of the Festival. Increasingly pieces were being chosen from the normal reportoire where formerly more specifically composed 'educational' music was the norm. More chamber music entries were evident. The works of British composers featured more prominently as did the compositions of 'local' composers, probably attributable to the influence of devolution and regionalism taking place in the last few years.

The spectrum of musical styles and diversity of music teaching which typifies youth music making today is nowhere more displayed than in the annual Festival of Music for Youth. Rigid categorization has been gradually broken down as it becomes increasingly difficult to make distinctions in contemporary music between 'serious' and 'pop'. Above all the emphasis is on the craft of performance. When children of varying ages and abilities play together in ensembles and orchestras the final presentation is the outcome of a richly varied experience. Musical performance, dance, drama and activities such as ice-skating and gymnastics offer unusual opportunities for cultivating qualities of self-discipline, leadership, group co-ordination and self-confidence. The act of performing a mental, emotional and physical activity within a strictly defined time limit is a phenomenon uniquely displayed in the performing arts. It is an aspect of education which deserves closer scrutiny.

Specialist schools for children showing exceptional musical ability

In 1962 the first school to be opened for children showing exceptional musical ability was a co-educational day school, the Central Tutorial School for Young Musicians, known since 1973 as the Purcell School. Beginning with only four pupils, it has now grown to over 100 students following a move to larger premises at Harrow-on-the-Hill. The school was founded to meet the needs of musically talented children from eight to eighteen years for whom normal school arrangements precluded the necessary time required for musical activity and, above all, for daily practice. A distinctive feature of the Purcell School is that each pupil is given the opportunity, if he so wishes, to have instrumental and other lessons with his own teacher outside the school, thus tapping the immense musical resources which London possesses. The timetabling of musical activity is such that lessons can be arranged in school hours if desired and practice times organized in school hours every day. Although some school bursaries are awarded to children who display particular musical giftedness, many local authorities also assist students with the necessary grants (Taylor 1973).

The Yehudi Menuhin School at Stoke d'Abernon is a co-educational boarding school which Menuhin established in 1963 to train young children from eight to eighteen years who show musical promise. Here instrumental instruction consists usually of two hours' tuition a week and a special feature of the Yehudi Menuhin School is the provision made for children to practise under supervision. In addition to the normal curriculum of any school which must prepare pupils for the examination requirements of 'O' and 'A' levels, pupils can study dancing, acting and a variety of handwork, including sculpture and modelling.

Chetham's Hospital School of Music at Manchester, in 1969 became the first *national* institution for young talented musicians. It is a co-educational boarding and day school where children of exceptional musical ability are enabled to pursue specialized training as an integral part of the school curriculum. The transformation of a Bluecoat School for Boys into a co-educational music school originated just after the Second World War when it undertook to provide choristers for Manchester Cathedral. This resulted in the acceleration of the development of both vocal and instrumental activities at the school. In 1969, with increased financial support, the first fully musical intake of fifty pupils arrived. At this point the school became co-educational and boarding accommodation was offered to enable children to take up places from every area of the country. Of the 275 pupils at least eighty-three per cent receive support from their local authorities. Aged between seven and nineteen years, the only requirement for entry is that of high musical potential. Two instruments are studied with twice weekly instruction for the first study and once weekly for the second. Similar to the Yehudi Menuhin School, supervised practice is an important feature of the programme. An advantage of being sited in Manchester is that the school has strong links with the Royal Northern College of Music, the Hallé Orchestra, the BBC Northern Orchestra and the University Music Department.

A recent addition to this category of specialist schools is the comprehensive Pimlico School which makes special provision for music. From September 1971 an intake of fifteen children was especially selected for their musical ability and offered the regular curriculum as part of a special timetable which includes at least ten periods of music a week. The school also acts as a music centre for the Inner London Education Authority schoolchildren for regular weekend music tuition and is the home of the London Youth Symphony Orchestra and the London Schools Symphony Orchestra and Concert Band. This pioneering project represents the first British attempt to emulate the examples of Eastern European countries in providing intensive musical training within the state system.

Wells Cathedral School is an independent, co-educational day and boarding school of about 600 pupils which dates from the thirteenth century. In 1969 the school became co-educational and, in the following year, after consultation with the Arts council, LEAs and London Music Colleges, it launched a scheme for gifted violinists. Providing places initially for twelve pupils, the scheme was extended in 1974 to include cellists, following a grant of £25,000 from the Leverhulme Trust. The string teaching scheme is linked with the Guildhall School of Music and Drama under the supervision of Professor Yfrah Neaman and Amaryllis Fleming. To provide for a suitably equipped music school and for the purchase of instruments, the Calouste Gulbenkian Foundation, Pilgrim Trust and other trusts gave grants totalling £32,000.

Pupils fall into three distinct categories according to their musical requirements. 1. Specialists, for whom a special timetable is devised and who receive two hourly lessons a week. These pupils are expected to make music their career. 2. Serious, who also have a timetable which permits them to spend two or three hours a day on music with one weekly instrumental lesson. 3. Choristers, who with a special timetable are placed in the same form as specialists and receive concentrated training in singing and sight-reading from the Cathedral music staff. The specialist music scheme at present applies only to string players yet there is a large music staff providing tuition in woodwind, brass, piano and harpsichord, guitar and composition. Apart from the Cathedral choir there are the school choir and choral society, three orchestras, six chamber groups and woodwind and brass ensembles.

Like Chetham's School, the St. Mary's Junior Music School, which became a specialist school in 1972, originated from its choir school function for St. Mary's Cathedral, Edinburgh. It is the first school in Scotland designed to give schoolchildren the intensive training which is considered to be vital to the full development of musical talent.

For many, the important advantage of all these schools is seen to be in the provision of *daily* music (Taylor 1973). Allowing for the ever increasing expansion of music centres in London and the provinces many music educators still feel that the particular needs of musical children can only be fully met by providing the opportunity to attend specialized schools such as these.

Schools with a traditional bias towards music: choir schools

Presiding over music in cathedrals and churches on a national advisory basis is the Royal School of Church Music (RSCM). Founded in 1927 by Sir Sydney Nicholson, a former organist at Westminster Abbey, the RSCM gives musical assistance to its affiliated churches, colleges and schools. Among its activities are courses given to clergymen, organists, choirmasters and choristers. For the latter, since 1965, the RSCM has conducted a Chorister Training Scheme with a series of graded tests, awarding insignias for each level of attainment. It is thus the equivalent of the Associated Board of the Royal Schools of Music in being a national co-ordinating and examining body and a means of maintaining standards in church music. It is also responsible for organizing a specialized type of inter-school festival for school choirs which is confined mainly to boys' preparatory and public schools and held at various cathedral and college venues.

Of the fourteen secondary and twenty-one preparatory schools which serve cathedral or collegiate foundations, many are independent and others have received a direct grant, like Bristol, Worcester and Hereford cathedral schools. In the present climate of instrumentally biased music making, the tradition of cathedral choirs might appear anachronistic, with their daily practices and sung services on six out of seven days. There has been considerable speculation and debate about the future of choir schools since the Education Bill of 1976 withdrew the direct grant and compelled schools to become either fully independent or wholly comprehensive. The clause prohibiting pupil selection on the basis of special aptitudes was amended to exempt music and dance schools from this ruling. However, choir schools could also justify their claim to making similar provision for musically talented children whose primary instrument is the voice.

Already some interesting developments are taking place. Wells Cathedral School has for the last eight years incorporated highly specialized instrumental schemes into its musical activities, in addition to its traditional choral emphasis. Southwell Minster Church of England (aided) Grammar School in 1976 became a comprehensive school of 1,210 children, brought about by incorporating a nearby Church of England voluntary controlled secondary modern school. The new co-educational school still maintains a junior department of forty places, admitting boys aged eight on a national basis solely by reference to musical ability. Thus, the tradition of training, educating and boarding cathedral choristers still continues.

If the Southwell Minster pattern is adopted by other schools there are challenging prospects for the future development of former choir schools. The introduction of girls into former all male institutions could raise problems as well as opportunities. Will cathedrals still maintain the hitherto unique sound of the all male choir possessing the tone quality associated with boy treble voices or will cathedral choirs gradually be composed of singers from both sexes? An opportunity presents itself for introducing a flexible choice of personnel in order to achieve a variety of choral sound, e.g. male, female, or mixed choirs. Varying tonal effects could be produced by gradual experimentation. For example, by arranging choirs antiphonally so that a contrasting permutation of tone qualities was achieved in the course of a service, greater choral contrast could result. It remains to be seen if these opportunities are taken up or ignored.

Many might be anxious to preserve the choral *status quo* for opinions have been voiced that English church music based on its cathedral choirs is a distinctive English contribution to the arts in general and that, in some ways, it parallels the development of the opera houses in Germany.

Nevertheless, the specific choral tradition associated with English church music is reliant on a continuing source of boy sopranos. Even if this source were to remain constant, the preservation of a choral style as a museum piece could be as inappropriate today as it would have been in the past.

Chapter 4

The growth of musicianship

Knowledge comes, but wisdom lingers.

TENNYSON

The curriculum

Values

A brief outline of music's historical role in the curriculum was presented in chapter 1. From this account it is evident that through the centuries emphasis has been placed at different times on varying aspects of musical behaviour, for example, on singing in the nineteenth century and on musical appreciation in the 1930s. At times the study of music appeared to be valuable mainly as a means to achieve goals unrelated to music education, such as in Roman times when considered as an aid to the practice of oratory and its function as a moralizing force in nineteenth-century England.

Extra-musical grounds such as these have often been the main justification for music's place in the curriculum. Particular importance has also been attached to extrinsic values such as music's socializing aspect, the encouragement it gives to the development of sound working habits and its effect as a vitalizing force in school life. Such claims could equally be made for other curriculum subjects. On the other hand, a sole emphasis on the intrinsic value of music in providing an 'aesthetic' experience, might well be to oversimplify the case. The justification for music's inclusion in the timetable rests neither on one nor the other but on a combination of both extrinsic and intrinsic values, as expressed by Brocklehurst (1971, p. 17).

> There is really no sharp dividing line between intrinsic and extrinsic values, between education in music and education through music; the development of musical responsiveness is both a means and an end.

Music study has a contribution to make to three broad areas of human development – the intellectual and emotional, the sensory-motor and the social.

Intellectual and emotional development

Hart (1974) describes the mature musician as one who has spent many hours in keen mental activity cultivating powers of concentration, perseverance, aural sensitivity and discrimination. Others have referred to the value of mastering a new language with a complex alphabet which must be read swiftly and translated into action (Gulbenkian 1965). Stress is laid on the processes of memory training, abstract thought through sonic thinking and on the experience of emotional and imaginative involvement. As a non-verbal form of expression music has been of extreme benefit in the education of the less able, the maladjusted and the handicapped. Many of these children may be unable or unwilling to express themselves by the standard verbal means.

Sensory-motor development
This area not only includes bodily response to music in the form of movement and dance, which benefits the a-rhythmic and physically uncoordinated but also the physical response involved in singing and playing. The muscular, co-ordinating and manipulative skills which translate the written symbol into sound are complex and considerable research has yet to be undertaken into this field of study.

Social development
The terms 'corporate spirit', 'orderly arrangement' and 'team work' have been frequently used in referring to music education and its benefits to school life (Schools Music Association 1962). It has also been described as 'a catalyst in the general life of the school' (Hart 1974). Corporate activity is an important part of music making which requires qualities of self-subordination and control, responsibility and precision. Although musical performance could not be described as unique among the arts in lending itself readily to group participation (for dance and movement also call upon these qualities), there might be some justification for labelling the high level of precision required in musical performance as 'unique'. Ragged imprecise singing or playing makes an immediate assault upon the ear yet it is possible for similar imprecision in dance to escape the untutored eye and does not result in any comparable degree of physical discomfort.

Goals
In order to establish clear and attainable goals, the music teacher plans a scheme of work which is in accordance with his own conception of music education. This approach is inevitably set within the framework of the teacher's particular philosophical outlook and tempered by the ethos of the social climate and the institution in which he teaches.

Leonard and House (1959, p. 100) in their comprehensive work on the foundations and principles of music education, give the following guidelines:

> The purpose of musical educators must be to develop the innate musical responsiveness of every individual to the highest possible level and to nurture and expand his potential for aesthetic experience.

In concise terms, Rainbow (1968) suggests that the teacher of music should be aiming for three ideals: that children should be encouraged to be musically articulate, musically literate and musically responsive.

Curriculum objectives

In order to pursue the above goals there is a need to make an analysis of the many elements of musical experience and their related curriculum objectives. For clarity, two writers particularly stand out for their use of diagrammatic form to show the diverse yet interrelated components of musical behaviour. Brocklehurst's musical communication chain (1971, p. 99) shows the productive, reproductive and receptive elements of music and the skills into which they are subdivided:

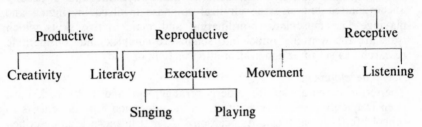

FIGURE 1   Brocklehurst's musical communication chain.

The interrelated nature of these elements is explained by the use of the word 'chain'. Both composer and performer need 'literacy', the one for recording, the other for interpreting. As a physical response 'movement' involves both reproductive and receptive elements. By linking 'listening' and 'creativity', the chain would be completed, for 'listening' not only influences all the skills but, in turn, is influenced by them.

In a publication specifically directed to teachers in primary schools Hart (1974, p. viii) shows, in the following diagram, the spectrum of activities which is considered to be integral to the music curriculum. Again the use of a circular format clarifies the relationships between the various musical elements. The detailed suggestions which are given although directed to the primary school curriculum could equally well serve as a basic guide to formulating curriculum objectives in the secondary school.

In fostering musical development two points are constantly emphasized:

1   The importance of balance in the curriculum.
2   The interrelationship and interdependence of each activity within the total musical experience.

In general, publications on music education fall into two categories. There are those which, in treating the philosophy and psychology of music tend to confuse and bemuse the reader by inconsistent use of terminology. The second category consists of publications which are specifically directed at general teachers in primary schools and, as such, are basic primers. Clear in their function, this kind of publication sets out

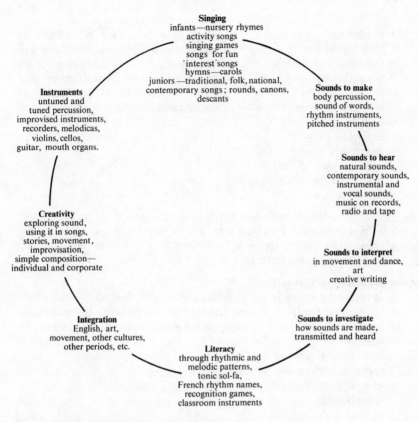

Singing
infants—nursery rhymes
activity songs
singing games
songs for fun
'interest'songs
hymns—carols
juniors—traditional, folk, national,
contemporary songs; rounds, canons,
descants

Sounds to make
body percussion,
sound of words,
rhythm instruments,
pitched instruments

Sounds to hear
natural sounds,
contemporary sounds,
instrumental and
vocal sounds,
music on records,
radio and tape

Sounds to interpret
in movement and dance,
art
creative writing

Sounds to investigate
how sounds are made,
transmitted and heard

Literacy
through rhythmic and
melodic patterns,
tonic sol-fa,
French rhythm names,
recognition games,
classroom instruments

Integration
English, art,
movement, other cultures,
other periods, etc.

Creativity
exploring sound,
using it in songs,
stories, movement,
improvisation,
simple composition—
individual and corporate

Instruments
untuned and
tuned percussion,
improvised instruments,
recorders, melodicas,
violins, cellos,
guitar, mouth organs.

FIGURE 2   Hart's musical relationships.

sharply defined objectives yet often only touches upon the more philosophical issues of the musical process.

It is therefore particularly relevant to describe a seminal publication which, in its detailed application of general learning theories to musical study, has wide implications for musical pedagogy at all levels. In the last decade, music educators have begun to apply Bloom's *Taxonomy of Educational Objectives* (1956) to their own field. Regelski (1975, pp. 207–13), however, has gone further than a general identification and use of the cognitive, affective and psycho-motor headings. He has expanded the number of classifications in the 'cognitive' domain and examined the hitherto neglected 'psycho-motor' domain in greater detail, as below.

Cognitive behaviours (covert)
   1 to perceive
   2 to comprehend
   3 to analyse

4 to identify
5 to differentiate
6 to compose or match
7 to synthesize
8 to apply abstractly
9 to evaluate or judge
10 to elaborate
11 to decide
12 to identify or empathize
with, or respond contem-
platively to in terms of
concepts.

Cognitive behaviour is defined as understanding, knowledge, conceptualization. It also involves percepts conditioned by unique factors and even by certain affects such as moods and emotions.

As examples of 'overt' cognitive behaviours in musical terms in (1) the students would locate phenomenon by bar number in the score; in (2) he would remember and reiterate information; and in (3) extract musical elements from the given context.

Affective behaviours (covert)
1 to respond intuitively
2 to interpret freely
3 to prefer
4 to enjoy
5 to characterize in terms of 'feeling'
6 to create or organize subjectively
7 to choose on the basis of 'feel'

Affective behaviour (Subjective responses) are accompanied or determined by certain concomitant emotional tones or states.

Psychomotor behaviours (covert)
1 to attend to cues
2 to imitate and to repeat
3 to monitor oneself
4 to follow instructions
5 to fixate through practice
6 to refine
7 to co-ordinate series of cues and acts
8 to acquire speed
9 to lessen time
10 to perfect
11 to hear inwardly

Psychomotor behaviour is concerned with the development of neuromuscular co-ordination necessary for skilled behaviour such as musical performance.

Regelski points out that in categories (6) and (8) fine muscle control is also a matter of physical maturity. He also draws attention to the fact that psychomotor development is characterized by high points, low points, phases and emphases, spurts and plateaux, a process comparable with biological growth.

In planning the curriculum Regelski draws the reader's attention to the need for balance between all three domains and to the interrelationships between them. Thus 'cognitive' objectives may be the means to 'affective' goals, 'affective' goals the means to 'cognitive' goals and so on.

In curricula where a predominating emphasis is put on musical performance there is always the danger of overbalance towards the psychomotor domain. As Regelski points out (1975, p. 218):

> Students involved in the acquisition of performance skills should be consistently confronted with cognitive and affective behaviours in an attempt to make them better able to understand the what, why and how of their performance ... without such cognitive and affective behaviour, psychomotor behaviour becomes meaningless, futile, unproductive, and often self-defeating.

The listed behaviours, initially 'covert', result in the following 'overt' behaviours:

> *verbalizing*—speaking, writing
> *making* — composing, arranging, rearranging, notating or
>   adapting
> *performing* — playing, singing, conducting, moving or dancing

And it is from these 'overt' behaviours or learning outcomes that the curriculum can be the more readily and effectively evaluated.

Instructional objectives

Instructional objectives can be defined as the day-to-day activities of the classroom, namely the activity and learning situations in which the 'concepts' of music are fostered.

Musical concepts fall broadly under the following headings:
> sound   rhythm   pitch   harmony   timbre
> dynamics   form   texture   style   tempo

and are taught through a process of musical learning involving:
> performing (reading, writing, playing, singing, moving)
> discriminating
> feeling
> knowing

Closer study of the Regelski analysis could be of considerable value to instrumental teachers, lecturers and class teachers in planning for greater variety and balance within the teaching period and in long term curriculum planning. At the same time, research areas have been opened up in all three domains which would merit further study and application.

Major influences on the curriculum

The foregoing has concentrated on the components of the curriculum from broad goals to specific instructional objectives. This section attempts to describe how the music curriculum has been influenced by developmental studies; research into music psychology; and the trend towards greater 'creativity' in learning. Finally the section focuses on the work of three individual music educators whose teaching methods have had a major impact during the last decade.

Developmental studies and their implications for musical learning

Developmental psychology is a fairly young discipline within the framework of general psychological studies. In the United Kingdom Bowlby's research studies and those undertaken at the Tavistock Clinic are credited with much of the pioneering groundwork into this area of child development (Sants and Butcher 1975, p. 9).

Within the last fifteen years it is the particular contribution of the Swiss psychologist Jean Piaget and his American counterpart Jerome Bruner which have been influential in the pre-school and primary areas. Their investigations into the early years of child development have been extensively applied, particularly work on the acquisition of language skills and concept formation (Sants and Butcher 1975). Already the extent of this influence can be seen in the primary music curriculum with its use of terms and materials analogous to those used in language and reading development. This is exemplified in the design of core curricula for primary schools which includes aids such as pre-readers, concept builders and games for visual discrimination (Kendell 1975). Leonard and House (1972) state that, through Piaget, music educators have been persuaded that the development of musicianship and aesthetic sensitivity should begin in early childhood and that it is accordingly in the nursery school, kindergarten and primary school where music provision should receive the highest priority.

Three other psychologists whose contributions to the theory of learning are seen to have potential application to music learning have also been identified. Skinner's emphasis on the need for constant and immediate reinforcement through the use of teaching machines could be highly relevant to certain aspects of music teaching. In traditional teaching immediate reinforcement is often absent. Teaching machines could also be extremely useful for self pacing in a subject where previous musical background, aptitude and rate of learning vary markedly from one individual to another. The programming of learning essential for the teaching machine would ensure a more scrupulous study of curriculum and instructional objectives and a more detailed examination of those musical behaviours which most characterize the skilled and sensitive musician.

Ausubel has been concerned to rescue verbal learning from its present disrepute. He has defined the distinction between reception and discovery learning and between rote and meaningful learning by emphasizing that both reception and discovery learning can be meaningful or that both may be rote. What determines the nature of the learning is whether the learner has a set to relate what is learned to an existing cognitive structure and whether there is potential meaning in the learning task. Application of Ausubel's theory could result in a significant inprovement in the learning and retention of musical information in general music classes, theory and history at secondary and advanced levels.

The psychologist Gagné has identified eight sets of learning conditions:

1 signal learning	5 multiple discrimination
2 stimulus response learning	6 concept learning
3 chaining	7 principle learning
4 verbal associate learning	8 problem solving

Again this analysis of learning conditions could provide music educators with a deeper insight into the process of learning and its possible application to music learning.

Research into the psychology of music

The preceding account has been concerned with developmental studies which are beginning to influence the music curriculum and to identify potential areas of study relevant to music learning. Music psychology is a relatively young discipline and so the next few paragraphs provide a brief historical background to this speciality before proceeding to an assessment of the current situation.

Two questions have tended to dominate the research work of music psychologists in the relatively short history of this area of study: is musical capacity composed of several specific abilities or is it a unified phenomenon and does musical capacity result principally from native endowment or from musical experience?

Of the principal protagonists, Seashore viewed musical talent as a hierarchy of separate musical capacities and his ability tests were constructed on this hypothesis. Mursell (1937 and 1948) is associated with the opposite view, the 'gestalt' theory where musical capacity is seen to be a unified whole. It was Lundin (1953) who first applied general psychological principles to the musical process. Describing himself as an 'interbehaviourist' he defined musical ability as a number of acquired interrelated behaviours built up through the process of individual organisms interacting with musical stimuli. He thus brought music psychology into line with current psychological thought and the use of the terms 'stimulus' and 'response' became common in describing the musical process. Regarding the question of whether musical ability is inherited or acquired, Lundin believed that musical responses were acquired yet did not deny that some people appear to be more biologically predisposed to respond to musical stimuli than others. Later Bentley (1966, chapter 8) concluded from the results of his control tests that musical abilities appear to be largely innate, a view shared by Shuter (1968, chapter 18) who discovered that musical ability tends to run in families and to appear early in life.

It is not surprising, therefore, that considerable research time has been devoted in recent years to the construction and refining of musical ability tests as a means of identifying musical talent as early as possible. In this country, the development of musical ability tests has been undertaken by Bentley (1966). Unlike the previous tests of Seashore and the British pioneer Wing, Bentley's tests have been specifically designed for children under the age of 11. In local authority areas where resources and peripatetic teaching are at a premium Bentley's tests are the most widely used. However, to view ability tests as having one sole function would be to neglect their wider value. The nature/nurture debate has moved toward the detailed study of environmental and experiential factors in human behaviour and the divisions between environment and heredity show a more complex interface. Thus, the results from Bentley's own control tests have prompted many questions relating to the nature of musical behaviour and development and, by a multiplying effect, have drawn many music educators into this field of study.

Some of the conclusions which emerged from Bentley's tests were:

that there is no significant difference between the sexes in musical ability;

that musical abilities in childhood appear to be associated only slightly with intelligence and the correlation is significant only between pitch discrimination and IQ;

that rhythmic memory is more highly developed at all ages of childhood than tonal memory; both appear to be more advanced than keen pitch discrimination and that the ability to analyse chords develops more slowly than the rest.

As a result of these findings, studies have since been undertaken into, for example, rhythmic ability (Thackray 1972) and pitch discrimination (Sergeant 1969). Perhaps the most comprehensive book on the psychology of music to be published recently is that by Davies (1978). One of the most valuable parts of this publication is the extensive bibliography which shows the dramatic increase in papers and articles published on this subject during the last thirteen years or so. From 1966, twice yearly conferences on Research in Music Psychology and Music Education have been held at the University of Reading. These have spawned, in their turn, a Society for Research in Music Psychology and Music Education, formed in 1973 as a propagating and disseminating centre for this field of study in the United Kingdom.

The 'creativity' element
Names such as Herbert Read (1958), Marian Richardson and Robin
Tanner serve as constant reminders of the quiet revolution which took
place in art education more than forty years ago. In the 1930s these
artists were instrumental in transforming school art from a technique-
bound and narrowly defined classroom discipline into the self-expressive
and varied activity which we today recognize as school art (Van der
Eyken and Turner 1969).

A substantial part of music consists of translating a printed score into
actual sound before the written note can become the 'art' form and this
interpretive process draws upon the expressive and imaginative powers of
the performer in a way which could equally well be called 'creative'. Yet
it is difficult to understand why the majority of teachers should take so
long to recognize the creative element (in the sense of original composition) as an important part of the music lesson. For it is only in the
last ten to fifteen years that a movement comparable to art has spread to
the primary school, and even more recently begun to influence the
secondary sector.

A timely combination of several factors appears to have encouraged
the eventual recognition of original musical composition as a vital
element in music education. Reference has already been made to the
work of Maxwell Davies which was publicized in the early 1960s. An
articulate spokesman himself, he effectively drew the profession's
attention to the parallels existing between the two art forms and
encouraged similar work. So too, in the early 60s the influence of Carl
Orff was being felt in this country. Perhaps more significant was the
impact of the 'Orff' instruments which, as exciting materials, brought to
the music lesson what Marian Richardson and others had introduced to
the art class many years earlier. The advantages of instruments such as
xylophones, glockenspiels and metallophones was that they were easily
played and transportable. Unlike the earlier percussion band (triangles,
drums, tambourines etc.) these 'pitched' instruments, like the recorder,
were able to provide both rhythmic and melodic interest. Interestingly the
chime bar, which the Rose-Morris Company introduced into the United
Kingdom back in 1951, only achieved real popularity and relevance as a
result of the Orff instrumentarium into which it was fittingly incorporated. The Orff instruments turned out to be the very resources needed
to spark off the 'creativity' movement.

Among the individuals who have given impetus to the extension of the
creativity movement into the secondary school are the composer/teacher
George Self and the philosophers John Dewey and Suzanne Langer.

George Self is one of an increasing group of composer/teachers whose
philosophy takes a much wider view of musical sound than his
predecessors and who endeavours to involve all children in musical
activities regardless of background or aptitude. Working from the
premise that it is not necessary to be able to read and write conventional

music before making it, Self encourages children to invent and construct their own instruments as a means of providing some kind of sound source, however primitive. The child is thus equipped to express music, become involved in group activities and develop self-confidence as a composer, performer and listener on his own terms.

In accordance with this philosophy, though not intended to supplant conventional means, Self has devised a notation whereby children may instantly record their ideas. Briefly, instruments are divided into categories according to their acoustical properties, for example sustaining instruments, such as violins and trombones; instruments with a dying sound such as the piano, chime bars, and cymbals; and instruments which can only make a staccato sound, for example, maracas and woodblocks. Appropriate symbols are then introduced to represent the various sound effects of which the instruments are capable (Self 1965).

sounds of natural length

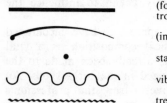

(for instruments like violins and trombones which can sustain a sound)

(instruments with a dying sound)

staccato

vibrato

tremolo

FIGURE 3   Self's notation for dividing instruments into categories according to their acoustical properties.

In the secondary school, music educators and the arts curriculum as a whole have been influenced by the philosophical writings of Dewey and Langer. This is evident in the work of Witkin (1974) who, with Ross (1975), investigated the status of arts subjects in the secondary school curriculum and in a subsequent music curriculum project. Dewey, many years ago, challenged the popular, romantic conception of musical art. This view, still widespread, tends to regard music as an aesthetic experience divorced from real life and an almost superhuman phenomenon. Dewey (1934) contended that aesthetic experience of music is closely related to ordinary experience. Indeed that the very rhythm of life, the struggle versus fulfillment, ebb/flow, tension/repose cycle is the whole basis for artistic experience.

Latterly the philosopher Suzanne Langer has been influential in focusing on the 'feeling' aspect of the mind rather than on the 'knowing' or 'cognitive' aspect. Langer's theory is that the 'feeling' nature of man reaches its fullest expression in the rhythm patterns and symbols of art (1967). Here the term 'feeling' is not to be confused with the symptomatic expression of emotions. For example, 'it may be the feeling of vitality, energy or somnolence, or any of the countless inward actions and conditions which are felt in the living fabric of mental life' (1967 p. 84). The influence of Langer's writings is seen in the increasing use of the terms 'expressive' or 'creative' arts, a 'feeling' response and 'self-realization'. In defining goals for the arts curriculum emphasis is being placed increasingly on the need to develop sensitivity, imagination and expression in each individual child and that this is a vital function of the secondary school educational system.

Three major music educators

Carl Orff, Zoltan Kodály and Shinichi Suzuki were concerned with the music education of every child, be he specially gifted or not. These three music educators stand out as influential figures who have had a major impact on the international scene during the last decade.

Carl Orff (1895–)

Orff's beginnings as a music educator spring from the same fertile period in the 1920s which produced such figures as Dalcroze, Laban and Wigman. Wishing to experiment with a new kind of rhythmical education in which music and movement were truly integrated, in 1924 Orff and Dorothea Guenther founded a school in Munich for gymnastics, music and dance. Like Dalcroze, this seminal work began, not with young children, but with students. The skills which Orff subsequently developed at the Guentherschule were based on rhythmic and melodic improvization which students were encouraged to foster through the use of simple instruments. To achieve success with this approach a need was felt for unsophisticated pitched percussion instruments which would be easy to play and to handle. This was how Carl Maendler, a piano and harpsichord maker, came to construct the first 'Orff Instrumentarium' working primarily from mediaeval and oriental prototypes. First to be constructed were xylophones, glockenspiels and metallophones, with wooden or metal bars, the name of the note being printed on each bar and built in soprano, alto, tenor and bass range. Then timpani, drums, tom-toms, gongs and cymbals were added. Stringed instruments such as cellos and violas da gamba were incorporated to provide a sustained drone bass. And through the help of Curt Sachs, a recorder consort was acquired by copying old models from the Berlin collections of old instruments (Orff 1964), a continental counterpart to the work of Arnold Dolmetsch in England.

The musical activity of the Guentherschule resulted in many educational demonstrations and publications. Orff was assisted at this time by Hans Bergese, Wilhelm Twittenhof and Gunild Keetman whose names were to be inseparably linked with Orff's future educational work. Much attention and publicity was given to the Guentherschule dance group which toured Germany and abroad, the dancers and musicians demonstrating their ability to exchange roles at will. Orff's plans to extend his educational work to young children and to publish his

Schulwerk-Music for Children were interrupted by the political events which brought Hitler to power.

However, his work was revived in 1948 when Bavarian Radio requested a series of school music programmes from him. So successful were these programmes that the outgrowth was the now familiar five volumes of Orff-Schulwerk published in 1950 and a factory, Studio 49, which was set up in response to the demand for instruments resulting from the broadcasts (Horton 1969). Rejuvenated by this radio project Orff realized that his previous work had neglected two essential elements, the 'singing voice' and the 'spoken word'. As a result the singing games, calls, chants, rhymes of young children at play were incorporated into what he now saw as a naturally integrated unity — elementary music, elementary speech and elementary movement. Using simple sequence forms such as ostinato and rondo, 'elementary' music was the term he used to describe something which was unsophisticated and essentially music which children could make themselves.

The first English translation of the five basic Orff-Schulwerk books was made by Doreen Hall and Arnold Walter for Canadian schools in 1958. This was eventually superseded in the United Kingdom by Margaret Murray's translation and adaptation in which she replaced German traditional material with appropriate British equivalents. The material of these five volumes is intended to serve as musical 'models' rather than pieces and the principal technique is that of using improvisation as the means of stimulating and developing musical imagination. Child developmental in sequence, the contents cover the following range:

Volume 1 the two-note 'cuckoo call' or falling minor third building up to the pentatonic scale. Rhythmic patterns from name calling, counting out rhymes, simplest children's rhymes and songs.
Simple forms: ternary, binary, rondo, canon, inversion, augmentation and diminution.

Volume 2 whole major scale with drone bass and tonic triad.

Volume 3 introduces dominant and subdominant ostinati and parallel chords.

Volume 4 introduces minor mode with drone bass.

Volume 5 minor mode with dominant and subdominant harmonies.

A practical handbook has subsequently been published (Keetman 1974) which provides teachers with a practical guide to the elements of Orff-Schulwerk. Rhythmic 'building bricks' is the term given to rhythmic patterns formed from speech patterns contained in rhymes, songs and names. These units are then expressed through bodily movement, hand clapping, thigh or knee slapping, finger snapping, feet stamping, walking, running, skipping etc., and then transferred to instrumental playing. The natural progression is therefore voice – body — instrument.

Orff-Schulwerk was not conceived as a rigid educational method but as an approach to music which could develop and incorporate new ideas as long as the guiding principles were fully understood and implemented. Since 1963 new instruments such as the dulcimer, psaltery and other folk instruments have been added. The emerging importance of the recorder in the instrumentarium has come from its great value as an instrument, which like the voice, can sustain a melodic line.

In 1951 Gunild Keetman joined the staff of the Mozartium in Salzburg to run Schulwerk courses. This led in 1961 to the founding of the Orff Institute. Training lasting from one to three years as well as short courses are held here and the Institute has effectively spread knowledge of the work to Europe and the rest of the world. In the United Kingdom the pioneering work of Margaret Murray must receive special acknowledgement. Her name is associated with the dissemination of Orff-Schulwerk through the Orff-Schulwerk Society, lectures, courses, articles and by the translations and adaptations of the basic material which she has made. Another contributing factor to the popularity of the Orff instrumentarium are the several companies which not only manufacture Orff instruments but also run courses both in the United Kingdom and in Germany. The influence of Orff-Schulwerk is now seen in the majority of publications directed at music teaching in primary schools. Increasingly too the use of Orff instruments is advocated in secondary school work for the opportunities they provide for self-expression and experimentation (Witkin 1974). However, the use of such instruments divorced from the philosophical context from which they spring can and often has led to abuse. This is why the underlying principles of the approach need to be properly understood before any such classroom work can be labelled 'Orff-Schulwerk'. In its free and improvisatory approach Orff-Schulwerk presents a challenge. It exercises and develops the teacher by demanding classroom organizational skills based on a thorough knowledge of Orff's particular philosophy of music education and a sound and thorough musicianship.

Zoltan Kodály (1882–1967)
Kodály was a composer and musicologist whose pedagogic achievements earned him the title 'educational revolutionary' (Russell-Smith 1969). His purposeful efforts to create a music education system from a foundation of Hungarian folk material were triggered off in the 1920s when Kodály reacted to the low level of musical taste and teaching which then prevailed. It was significant that, after a complex history of foreign domination, Hungary was only just beginning to be conscious of its own national identity and to value its own individual culture.

Kodály drew on the corpus of folk song which he, Bartok and others had collected and analysed over many years, to transform Hungarian music education into the integrated, organized system evident today. The school system comprises a network of general schools and singing primary schools. It was in 1950 that the first singing primary school was opened at Kecskemet and there are now more than 130 such schools. This outstanding achievement must be seen in relation to the size of the country and its population, an area roughly as large as Ireland with approximately ten million inhabitants. The musical standards of these special music schools have not only proved extremely high but it is also claimed that they have had a significant bearing on other areas of the curriculum (Sándor 1966).

The guiding philosophy underpinning the whole of Kodály's educational work was that music had an important part to play in society, in the life of children, youth and adults alike (Szönyi 1973). In his determination to raise the general level of musical taste and education, Kodály developed a method whereby musicianship and literacy are fostered through the voice, as the child's first natural instrument, based on a system of tonic sol-fa training. Acknowledging his debt to Curwen and his forerunners, Kodály devised a graded sequence of teaching materials drawn principally from folk music and his own ethnically inspired exercises which together make up the Kodály Choral Method (twenty-two books, written and compiled between 1941 and 1967). The aim of Kodály training is to cultivate the ear, what he referred to as the faculty of 'inner hearing', from the earliest stages through unaccompanied singing. At a later stage, when proceeding to instrumental tuition, children would benefit from being able to intellectualize the sound before producing it. He therefore insisted that piano accompaniments should be avoided at the primary level, for in being tuned by equal temperament a piano can neither correspond to the pure intonation of the voice nor to the inevitable fall in pitch which takes place over time in children's singing. Strongly objecting to the common tendency to overuse piano accompaniment, Kodály stressed that if one always uses crutches, one will in time be unable to walk without them. Thus, the instrument best fitted to accompany the human voice is another human voice and, as the only way to sing in tune is to relate one note to another, two-part singing is introduced at an early stage.

As it is the normal custom for the majority of Hungarian children to attend nursery schools before compulsory education begins at six, the music curriculum begins at the age of three. In the space of the next three years the children learn approximately seventy-five folk songs and singing games. Dalcroze movement and musical games involve them in stepping, tapping and clapping and accustom them to the concepts of dynamics and tempo change. From this sound base they are ready to begin musical reading and writing upon entry to primary school, following a curriculum which is again child developmental in sequence. As in Orff-Schulwerk the first interval to be identified is the children's chant of the falling minor third — 'soh-me'. So too, the initial scale is the pentatonic which is idiomatic to Hungarian folksong and considered by both Orff and Kodály to be most suitable for young children. In reviewing Curwen's tonic sol-fa method, Kodály adapted and made more flexible use of the hand signs but discarded the full notation. For example

$$\left| \text{d} \quad :\text{m.s} \,\middle|\, \text{r} \quad :\text{r.t,} \,\middle|\, \text{d} \quad :\!-\!\right\|$$

as rhythmic values can be shown just as easily by orthodox means. The use of numbers for the degrees of the scale, employed at one time in France by Galin, Paris and Chevé is introduced at a certain stage for the learning and singing of intervals and for indicating the bass, third or fifth in chords. An adaptation of Chéve's time names is also used for the initial stages of musical instruction and subsequently for identification purposes.

A comprehensive and detailed exposition of the principles of Kodály's method is to be found in Szönyi's publications (1973 and 1974) in addition to several Hungarian publications available in translation. The main features which distinguish this method from that of its tonic sol-fa predecessors are summarized as follows:

1   The early introduction of the staff, showing the relative positions of the sol-fa notes results in a dual, constantly reinforcing system, for example

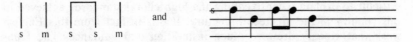

2   Curwen's vertical modulator is abandoned in favour of linear progression as shown in (1) and the 'pointing stick' is replaced by a 'flying note' used to describe melodic progression on the staff.

3   The teacher's constant aid, a tuning fork, ensures that at once or at any time when the staff is used, 'doh' is always given at the correct pitch. In this way a sense of absolute pitch is being fostered from the earliest stages.

4   The diversity of motor-sensory exercises from simple to advanced level develops rhythmic and melodic co-ordination. An example of such an exercise is one where a simple melodic progression is sol-fahed while a rhythmic phrase is tapped by the left hand and a different phrase by the right.

5   Although a common curriculum is followed, the 'Method' is sufficiently flexible to encourage teachers to be imaginative and to stretch their musicianship to its maximum potential. This is shown in the classroom or choir rehearsal when, for example, teachers use both hands to improvise two-part exercises.

6 Memorization is an integral part of Hungarian music education and it is to the memorized store of folk song that every new teaching element is related. For example when the interval doh-me is to be taught, reference is made to all the known folk songs which incorporate this interval in the first bar.

7 The continuity of the use of sol-fa extends from nursery school to advanced choir. At all levels, for the first 'sing through' of any work, sol-fa syllables are used.

In English-speaking countries knowledge of the Kodály Method has been disseminated by Young (1964), Russell-Smith (1969) and Vajda (1974). The most practical and relevant adaptation of this approach for British schools has been made recently by Russell-Smith (1977, 1978). In these books the author makes full use of British traditional material, including current playground games and chants, to produce a most effective combination of the Hungarian vocal approach with the instrumental, using those instruments (recorder and pitched percussion) most frequently found in British schools today. A publication by Choksy (1974) is extremely valuable for its comprehensive review of the adaptation of the method in countries outside Hungary. International appreciation of the Hungarian system has already led to the establishment of Kodály centres in the USA, Canada, Japan and Germany yet surprisingly no such centre has yet been established in the United Kingdom. This situation is difficult to explain when recalling the high choral standards achieved in this country in the nineteenth century. It was in fact from this English work that Kodály drew so much inspiration and guidance. The Hungarian influence has been felt in the regeneration of interest in the value of tonic sol-fa for young children, yet the full implications of applying this method at all levels have not received any marked attention. Kodály centres, as the Americans and Canadians appreciate, represent a way of disseminating a proven teaching method which focuses on aural work and vocal skills as the basis from which all musical activity should stem.

It is clear from the preceding accounts that the teachings of Orff and Kodály diverge in certain ways. The Hungarian system is taught as a Method (the term implies a measure of rigour) and its teaching sequence is strictly adhered to in fostering musical skills and literacy. Orff-Schulwerk, on the other hand, is freer, gives more emphasis to individual musical imagination and encourages improvisation as the means of developing it. Yet these two approaches to music education have much in common. Sharing the same background and philosophy, Orff and Kodály were both established composers with a concern for music education at all levels. Capitalizing on traditional material as the root source of musical learning each went back to first principles in formulating a child developmental learning sequence. Above all, their approaches share the common goal of providing every child with a dynamic musical experience based on a framework of sound musical and technical skills.

Shinichi Suzuki (1898–   )

The Japanese music educator Shinichi Suzuki began his famous 'Talent Education' movement in 1945, more commonly known in the western world as the 'Suzuki Teaching Method'. By this means thousands of Japanese children have learned to play the violin during their pre-school years on specially scaled down instruments from 1/16 to 1/2 size.

Talent Education, unlike the previous two approaches, is a private venture and forms no part of the state system in Japan. Neither is any form of selection involved, for Suzuki firmly believes that musicality is a human aptitude which can be nurtured from birth (Suzuki 1969, preface).

> Talent is no accident of birth. A newborn child adjusts to his environment in order to live and various abilities are acquired in the process

This is echoed in the following extract from Mills and Murphy (1974, p. 9)

> If all parents were awakened to the inherent nature of their children and provided them with an ideal environment all children would gain extraordinary ability ... education begins at birth

Suzuki observed how skilfully children learn their native language – chiefly by imitation and repetition. He then analysed the detailed process involved (Garson 1971) and applied this 'mother tongue' method to the teaching of the violin. Subsequently the same approach has been applied to the teaching of other stringed instruments, the piano, maths, art and English.

Suzuki pupils usually begin their violin lessons at three, sometimes earlier. From the beginning parents are essential contributors to the learning process and are encouraged to surround their children with good music, thereby creating the most favourable environment for musical learning. Usually the mother learns to play the violin before her child's first lessons begin. In this way the child is suitably motivated and encouraged to imitate not only the teacher but also the parent.

Suzuki regards two principles as essential to the success of his approach: first, the child must be helped to develop an ear for music and second, from the very beginning each step must be thoroughly mastered. A fixed course of ten books of pieces is strictly followed. Essential to the course are the accompanying records, for these present the models for children to assimilate before learning to play themselves. A 'plateau' system ensures that pieces are grouped on the same technical level, yet each introduces a different technical feature. Lessons provide a mixture of individual and group playing when children have an opportunity to play to each other, play in unison and take part in musical games. Great interest has been generated from films and television recordings which show Japanese children moving around while playing, changing places or bowing each others' violins.

From the earliest stages the greatest importance is attached to the following points:

1 thorough and religious learning;
2 memory training (reading is not introduced until the third or fourth year);
3 repetition (adults are often bored by this, yet forget that young children need and delight in repeating a skill once mastered);
4 good posture and movement patterns from the beginning of training.

Suzuki's Method first spread to the western world in 1958 when a Japanese student studying at Oberlin in Ohio showed a seven minute film of 1,000 Japanese children playing Bach's Double Violin Concerto. Such was the impact of this film that American and Canadian music educators were inspired to visit and study the Method in Japan. The first Suzuki visits to the USA began in 1964 and Talent Education, USA was established in 1967 (Mills and Murphy 1974).

It was not until 1970 that the Method was brought to Europe. In that year the tour of the United Kingdom attracted not only the interest of many music teachers but also substantial general interest through television and press coverage. As a result of this and subsequent tours, increased attention has been given to the possibilities and implications of teaching stringed instruments to pre-school children. This has been made possible by the availability of scaled-down instruments imported from various countries. The centre for Suzuki work in this country is the Rural Music Schools' Association. Here courses have been run on the Method and, in 1977, the RMSA completed a five year research programme into the Suzuki Method and its adaptation in the United Kingdom. This project was funded by the Leverhulme Trust Fund and Calouste Gulbenkian Foundation who jointly contributed £27,000 to cover the cost of training selected teachers, the associated field work and the necessary instruments and teaching material. Results from the Suzuki investigation (RMSA 1977) indicate that, by modifying the Suzuki Method to meet British conditions, applications of the basic principles would be most beneficial in schools. The need for modification is seen primarily in problems relating to parental involvement and the more regimented teaching approach which runs counter to current British educational practice.

Criticisms which have been levelled at certain features of the Method tend to reflect the western world's reaction to an approach rooted in a traditional Japanese culture. The Suzuki investigation again highlights certain criticisms discussed some years ago by Cole (1972) and particularly relate to teaching traditions and family structure, narrowness of repertoire and standardized interpretations, and emphasis on rote learning. It is easy to overlook the fact that this method was devised for *very* young children and that any learning approach must be seen in the context of its original application and development. The basic idea of attempting instrumental teaching with very young children is already being taken up by music teachers. An example of one such venture is a piano class for three and four-year-old children (Crump 1978). Undoubtedly this will lead to much more experimentation with instrumental teaching and the pre-school child, a hitherto neglected area.

Suzuki's rejection of the importance of heredity or musical endowment, however unscientific, shifts the accent towards motivation and human endeavour. This is fundamental to educational progress and, in Japan, the Method has produced astonishing results. Yet the total philosophy and underlying principles of Suzuki's teaching, as with those of Orff and Kodály, are all too often unappreciated, misunderstood or only partially applied. All three teaching approaches have much to offer. Until the United Kingdom can produce a music educator of equal stature, the music teaching profession would do well to give these three approaches to music learning the substantial study, adaptation and development which they merit.

Music's application and integration

The therapeutic imperative
Piaget's concern for the paramount needs of the individual child, the growth of child developmental studies, a consciously caring society — these are some of the factors which have focused attention on the specific needs of the maladjusted, the physically and mentally handicapped. The psychoanalytic studies of Anna Freud, Winnicott and of Erikson (1950) have highlighted the varying rates of individual growth seen at all stages of human development. Consequently, we have seen the waning influence of Gesellian normative studies and an increasing recognition of the individual's differing educational and social requirements.

A wide range of educational establishments now exists from schools for the severely subnormal to those for the highly talented. Remedial work has become a specialized branch of education, and therapy, particularly psychotherapy, increasingly common in hospitals and schools.

The value of the arts to this field of study has been inestimable. In the application of the arts to therapeutic work acknowledgement must be made to the pioneering work of figures such as Dalcroze (Dutoit 1971), Laban and Steiner (Foster 1977). More recently there has been increased interest in the therapeutic value of the arts for every individual, a movement which has received impetus from the studies and teaching of Peter Slade (1954) in educational drama, social drama and drama therapy.

Employing music in medical practice as a curative tool is by no means a modern innovation for, since ancient times, music has been used as an aid to healing in some form or other. That music therapy has now achieved professional status is largely a result of music's value during the last world war. The many benefits which it displayed in military hospitals, factories and stress situations led to increased scientific scrutiny in the post-war years.

Music is now used for therapeutic purposes in medicine either as a main factor of the method as in music therapy, as an adjunct to some form of physical treatment, i.e. occupational therapy, or as a relaxing or stimulating agent in recreational therapy. Scientific experiments have shown that music causes not only physical and psychical action but also chemical action. Studies of the physiological and mental effects of music on the body have demonstrated that, when listening to music, breathing is accelerated and its regularity decreased. The heart beat is usually quickened. Respiratory variations coincide with markedly differing effects on circulation, blood volume, pulse, blood pressure and metabolism. Inevitably, increased blood pressure results in a large supply of blood, bringing warmth and nutrition to the body. This in itself contributes to the restoration of the body to mental and physical health (Schneider 1964).

Specific applications of music in medical treatment have been described by Alvin (1966). To the individual the main psychological effects are found to occur in communication, identification, association, imagery, self-expression and self-knowledge. To the group the effects of music are contagious. Certain music provokes a feeling of harmony and orderly behaviour, other kinds can incite a general lack of control and disorder. Stimulating music has been found to increase verbalization and relaxing music has the opposite effect. In evoking physical response music stimulates action and movement to the extent that it also generates physical strength. Singing, as a physical response, has benefits to total health, particularly to respiratory and digestive functions.

Increasingly music therapy has been employed in the care of the mentally handicapped, the brain damaged, emotionally disturbed, mongoloid, autistic, psychotic and insane. It has been found to improve general condition, to increase learning capacity and to facilitate group relationships and group work. As a tool of communication, active involvement in music often increases the attention span and the ability to concentrate. For the hyperactive and volatile it may provide opportunities for practising self-control. Rhythmical work can also provoke the withdrawn and the lethargic to a quickened response and can be of great benefit to the mal-coordinated.

Work with autistic and psychotic children is considered to be a particularly specialized area and here considerable studies and application have been made by Nordoff and Robbins (1971 and 1975). Their approach has been to regard music therapy as a direct means of stimulating a child to communicate and relate to other people. In individual therapy the Nordoff and Robbins method encourages a child to beat a drum while the therapist improvises at the piano, attempting to establish some form of communication. This may begin by the therapist breaking through the child's obsessive drum beat with dissonant, irregular piano music before proceeding to changes of mood and dynamics and questions and answers in a form of musical conversation designed to encourage responsiveness. Akin to Orff's elemental approach, Nordoff and Robbins developed group activity through musical games or play-songs which incorporate the natural rhythm of speech, songs and physical action in a traditional folk tale setting. They have described their form of musical activity as part of a 'developmental social environment', a description which could also apply to the therapeutic work of Fairview State Hospital in California where Orff-Schulwerk has been used with young subnormal patients (Bitcon 1969).

Many mentally handicapped children have the added disability of associated physical handicaps. Here children may need extra assistance to help to alleviate some of the more severe physical problems. Bailey's (1973) work with mentally and physically handicapped children led him to provide and devise particular gadgets to overcome specific disabilities. To facilitate forearm rotation he invented a double-headed drum-stick; for wrist exercise a music box with a handle. Puppets were also used to provide similar incentives for moving fingers and toes. In all work of this kind it has been stressed that there is an inevitable balance to be made between the musical needs and the therapeutic needs of each individual. A child's total development and the maximizing of his growth potential must be constantly borne in mind in effectively combining education and therapy.

Music's value in the treatment of physical disorders is evident from its use as an occupational therapy. Dull exercises can be enlivened by suitably chosen musical accompaniment. It is a valuable rhythmic aid for exercising afflicted limbs and in assisting co-ordination. Learning to play an instrument is often the very incentive needed to exercise limbs which might otherwise atrophy. In orthodontics it has also been shown that wind instruments can strengthen lips as well as mouth muscles and speech defects are often seen to improve following a programme of singing lessons.

Music can also be a therapeutic agent in the treatment of sensory disorders such as deafness where vibrations can be felt through the resounding body of a piano, drum or autoharp. It has been found that children are very rarely one hundred per cent deaf and that they can be helped to achieve rhythmic speech patterns through preliminary work of this kind. Blow organs and melodica have proved beneficial to the deaf (Adams 1970). By means of breath control they are enabled to produce sound and play correct rhythms, to perceive the produced sound and be aware of distinct differences of pitch.

The first official course of training for music therapists began in the state of Michigan, USA, in 1944. In the United Kingdom, it was in 1958 just at the time when the age cohort was cresting that a group of musicians led by Juliette Alvin founded the Society for Music Therapy and Remedial Music. Now known as the British Society for Music Therapy its aim is to promote the use and development of music therapy in the treatment, education, rehabilitation and training of children and adults suffering from emotional, physical or mental handicap. Its membership is made up of therapists, musicians, teachers, psychologists, psychiatrists, parents and social workers. From 1961 to 1966 the Society initiated part-time experimental courses in music therapy which, in 1967, developed into the first full-time courses in this country, run in association with the Guildhall School of Music. There is now a department of Music Therapy at the Guildhall which runs a one year post-graduate course (LGSMT). Twelve places a year are available to graduate musicians. The course includes psychology and child development, psychology of music, human relationships, group dynamics and the study of mental, physical and emotional disorders. Practical work is undertaken in hospitals, special schools and clinics. Professional studies include instrumental tuition, improvisation, movement and keyboard musicianship.

The other well-established full-time course in the United Kingdom is that run by Sybil Beresford-Pierse at the Nordoff Music Therapy Centre in the Goldie Leigh Hospital for severely abnormal children. Pioneered by the late Paul Nordoff and Clive Robbins, this course is assisted by a grant from the Music Therapy Charity. As the piano is regarded as essential to the Nordoff and Robbins' approach, a professional standard of piano playing is expected from the twelve students accepted on the course each year. Improvisation is a key element in therapeutic technique and, in its widest sense, means an ability to use musicianship and training in an imaginative, exploratory and infinitely adaptable manner. This is seen to be necessary in searching for new ways of communicating with those who cannot communicate through conventional means. In the Nordoff and Robbins course, training in improvisation and in clinical practice is given simultaneously. A student therapist plays the piano and sings while another, acting as assistant, encourages the child to strike a variety of percussion instruments and to vocalize. As the lesson is in progress other students and instructors observe through a two-way mirror. The sessions are taped, analysed and discussed.

The practice of music therapy, although a growth area, is still in its infancy in this country and still has certain difficulties to overcome. Lying as it does in the difficult area between art and science, music therapy still has to win full recognition from a medical profession which is divided as to its merits. Nevertheless, the study and practice of music therapy has served to widen the professional repertoire of musicians. As Dr Donald Blair (1970) has stated:

We are concerned with a new function of music, of interest to anyone concerned with the health and welfare of people in need.

From the beginning of the 1970s, following North American example, advertisements for hospital music therapists have become increasingly common. Education authorities too, such as Oxfordshire, Solihull, the former West Riding and Bradford, have been forerunners in adding music therapists to their specialist services.

Perhaps the most recent application for therapeutic music has been in remedial work with children who, for a variety of reasons, might be regarded as dull or backward. Some children appear to be backward because they have missed important steps or processes through school absence of frequent changes of school. Others have emotional problems which hinder the expression of intelligence and there are also slow developers who appear to blossom only when they are ready (Dobbs 1966). In remedial classes the particular value of singing has been frequently stressed. Apart from its more obvious benefits to posture, breathing and general physiological processes, singing has been seen to lead to improvement in language, speech and reading skills (Ward 1973). The first major research project on musical activities with slow learning children was an eight year study called 'Music and the Slow Learner'. Directed by Dobbs and Ward at Dartington (where the first full-time course was also initiated in 1971) this project was sponsored by the Standing Conference for Amateur Music, funded by several grant awarding trusts and foundations and completed in 1976. Two publications (Ward 1976 and Hunt 1976) describe the investigation and teaching carried out in this project and demonstrate convincingly the value of musical activities both to the musical development and to the general development of slow learning and retarded children.

In the mid-sixties considerable publicity was given to the work of Glenn Doman at the Institute for the Development of Human Potential in Philadelphia where he taught brain damaged children to read. As a consequence he developed a reading programme for unimpaired children aiming at a much younger age level than previously had been thought possible (Doman 1965). In time it is probable that the practice of music therapy will yield similar outcomes. Some of these may have considerable relevance for the normal music curriculum and for the music education of the pre-school child.

Music's integration with movement, dance and drama

So far the term 'therapy' has been used to describe music's application as a tool in a curative or remedial process. In recent years therapy has come to have a wider meaning. 'Play' has been the subject of considerable research and the value of 'play therapy' generally recognized. The benefits to individual development through improvisation and spontaneity in structured play situations has led to the therapeutic use of the arts as a catharsis or outlet for personal expression. Child art has already had a head start in establishing this facet or function of the arts. In its wake now follow the integrated arts of music, dance and drama and the recognition of the opportunities which they offer for individual response and personal development.

As music, dance and drama have a natural affinity, so are sound and movement inextricably linked. Whether sound preceded movement or whether movement preceded sound is hypothetical. Suffice it to say that they are unified elements and the sounds and movements of the body, for example in heart beat, breath, vocal utterance or foot stamping, stem from an over-riding rhythmic impulse.

If 'sound' is the language of music, then 'movement' could be described as the language of dance. Drama as an all-embracing art form is expressed through the combination of both sound and movement. The natural affinities linking the three art forms and their primary source might be shown in the following manner:

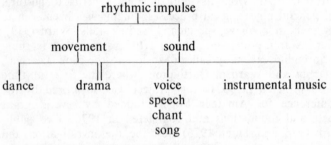

FIGURE 4   Natural affinities between art forms.

These links are demonstrated most clearly in children's traditional songs and games. Action songs, dancing and singing games contain all the elements of music, dance and dramatic action as a primitive, root form of cultural expression. Concerned with reality, ritual, magic and the forces of nature, they portray social events, religious and seasonal customs. The rhythm of life is enacted through the cycle of a year. Goodridge (1970, p. 1) defines drama as, 'Drama is action, movement, a form of physical, including vocal, expression'. For Slade (1954, p. 25) drama means 'doing and struggling'. Undoubtedly, in embryonic form, the elements of dramatic action found, for example, in 'Briar Rosebud was a Pretty Child' or 'Oranges and Lemons' fulfil these criteria.

Movement and dance
The term 'movement' has been used up to now to describe an element fundamental to both dance and drama. Yet there is a tendency for the terms 'movement' and 'dance' to be used interchangeably in describing expressive physical activity and, as a consequence, any account of this area faces difficulty in using terms with precision. The difference,

according to one authority (Lofthouse 1970, p. 4) is that 'dance is a rhythmicising of a body activity' and, wherever relevant, the term will be used in this context.

The early 'music and movement' broadcasts were conducted by Dalcroze's pupil Ann Driver who, with her sister Ethel, was instrumental in maintaining the impetus of Dalcroze's teaching for some considerable time. Eurhythmic principles put the stress on the musical side of the partnership. Musical concepts, analysis and appreciation by this method are assimilated through bodily movement and dance. Basic rhythms such as marching, walking, jumping, running, skipping are taught through suitably improvised piano music for it is advocated (Driver 1951, p. 43) that 'when teaching the simplest elements in music always associate them in the children's mind with a musical idea'. In teaching rhythm, strong accents are shown by a movement of the hand or head, children's names are examined and their rhythm pattern played. The spacing of scales is shown in human form as the height and depth of sound. Musical phrasing and structure are also expressed in compositional dance and visual terms.

For many years music and movement was based on the principles described above. By the late 1950s, however, the influence of Dalcroze was waning and the music and movement class from this time became primarily influenced by the teaching of Rudolf Laban. The impact of Laban on the physical education profession was considerable from the time when he became resident in England in 1938 until after his death twenty years later. It is generally acknowledged that the Laban Art of Movement Centre has made a significant contribution to maintaining the momentum of his teaching in this country.

Concerned with the fundamental significance of movement in the development and expression of personality, Laban saw movement as a prime educational force. He emphasized the qualitative aspects of movement and subjected it to systematic description. This 'movement analysis' provided working principles for all physical education specialists. In general terms, there is an identification of several aspects of movement. Thus there are 'qualitative aspects', which are described as the four motion factors of 'time', 'weight', 'space' and 'flow'; and spatial aspects which are concerned with personal space, common or general space, the different levels where movement takes place and the differing shapes of which the body is capable. 'Relationship aspects' deal with movement made as an individual, with a partner, or in a group. Lastly, 'bodily aspects' focus on anatomical actions, such as bending, stretching or twisting; types of action such as balancing or spinning; the contribution of different parts of the body such as those which move and those which support; and the order in which the various parts move. In sum, there is constant consideration of 'what is moving, how it is moving, where it moves and any relationship involved' (Department of Education and Science 1972b, p. 16).

The progress of the Music and Movement school broadcasts has been a useful barometer in terms of changing trends and influences. 'Movement and Music' as a new title was soon superseded by 'Movement, Mime and Music'. Inevitably there has been a shift in emphasis from music to movement as Laban's principles became universally adopted in educational circles from the later 1950s onwards. At the same time, it must be acknowledged that many of Dalcroze's ideas have been assimilated over the years and, like the accepted use of worthwhile music in movement work, have become implicit to the main stream of educational practice. Reference is made in a later chapter to the neglect of movement training in the music curriculum in higher education. There is now a far greater chance of children being introduced to the elements of music through movement by the physical education teacher than by the music teacher. Fortunately, through the efforts of Elizabeth Vanderspar, a full-time Licentiate Diploma Course in Dalcroze Eurhythmics has once again become available at the Roehampton Institute of Higher Education (an internal course was run at the Royal College of Music for many years). Introductory courses are also available at the City Literary Institute and at Goldsmiths' College. Dance educators stress the need for teachers of music and dance to work together in this area (Bruce 1972).

> I would like to see the teacher of music knowing more about movement as we come to work more closely together. A teacher of music might often use movement as the teacher of dance uses sound, to assist understanding, to enrich and to enhance.

In the teaching of movement dance the physical education teacher can use music in several ways (Lofthouse 1970, p. 50).

> Music is probably most widely used in educational dance as a stimulus, an exciter to action, where the rhythm dictates the dynamics and the melody the shape of the movement.

It also has the effect of stimulating the imagination of both pupil and teacher and of providing a structural framework for the teacher's ideas. The use of sound as a stimulus offers a range of vocal, bodily and instrumental sounds. In vocal sound, experimentation can be made with vowel sounds, consonants, words and phrases; body percussion can include finger clicking, hand clapping, thigh slapping, feet stamping; and instrumental sounds are easily and directly obtained from percussion instruments such as drums, tambours, tambourines, castanets and cymbals. Juxtaposing staccato sound with sustained sound forms part of a whole range of discriminatory training in variations of pitch, tone, volume and duration.

Sound as an accompaniment can assist in the execution of a movement, i.e. as an indicator of action. It assists propulsion, particularly in the learning of a movement sequence which demands repetition, a work dance for example. Usually it is the teacher who provides the instrumental sound, yet Bruce (1970) has pointed out that the most natural fusion of sound and movement occurs when a child dances to his own instrumental accompaniment.

Music may be used for atmosphere or for background. A mood can be set or coloured by the judicious choice of music which does not have direct control over the movement itself. In the use of composed music skilful selection of taped passages often provides more flexibility than records. In this respect there is a distinct value in the use of school broadcasts. Here, specially arranged music is played by first-rate artists and the producers have unlimited library resources for choosing suitable material.

Another aspect of dance in which music is important is that of the traditional or folk variety. These dances can often be quite freely adapted before more complex dance patterns are learnt. In an integrative approach to other subjects such as geography, or history, traditional and folk dance can illuminate these studies in an appropriate context.

Drama
The value of 'dramatic' play has been clearly expressed by McLellan (1970, p. 28).

> It was found that by having a sympathetic understanding of a child's dramatic play and a wide knowledge of the needs of the child at each stage of his development an adult can help a child to play a role which he has formerly avoided and can help him to find courage to meet new situations in group and individual play.

Peter Slade has extended this concept of dramatic play into the school curriculum at all levels. On the use and importance of sound as a stimulus to dramatic work, especially in the early stages, he states (Slade 1954, p. 94):

> On the whole too much stress is laid on meaning and too little on sound. Meaning is of the realm of intellect, sound is of the realm of emotion and it is because most adults cannot stand much of what we call 'noise' that we tend to stifle a great deal of experiment in sound. This prevents emotional and aesthetic development to some extent and hinders the growth of love of sound.

Sound's use as a stimulus to dramatic play is very similar to its use in dance. Simple sound effects such as the beating of a tambour or ringing of a bell can stimulate imaginative associations. It can also be used for incidental sound effects. Goodridge (1970) describes how sound can be explored from four different sources — physical, domestic, percussion, and conventional instruments. This approach is often used in the exploratory stages of music teaching and, as such, can be reinforcing to both art forms.

Slade (1954, p. 165) describes how the use of instrumental sound and quality can act as a subtle influence on speech, by using for example the sustained vowel sounds reproduced on a violin or bell and consonants on a drum or tambourine. Improvements in speech quality such as articulation, enunciation, projection and cadence have been seen to result from the influence of music's rhythmic and expressive elements.

Music is an aid to dramatic atmosphere, a mood setter. These values have been widely appreciated in film, theatre, radio and television.

As an idea source, ballads and work songs often provide the necessary impetus for characterization and dramatic situations. Music's role is seen to be important for rhythmic purposes, for atmosphere, and its assistance in expressing ideas more fully (Wiles and Garrard 1957, p. 92).

It gives meaning and rhythm to the most meaningless of actions. It uninhibits.

The application of music, in the ways which have been described, can be said to heighten or intensify the experience by exaggerating the other art form. The same thing happens when the dance element is added to drama (Goodridge 1970, p. 2).

Dance makes more obvious use of regular metric rhythm, locomotion and elevation than pure drama and exaggeration of normal gestures with turns and changes of level.

It is interesting that Wiles and Garrard refer to their work in educational drama as 'Movement and Mime to Music'. They see a very functional role for dance in working with adolescents who can express themselves through this form without the encumbrance of reading from a script.

Operas and cantatas for children
No account of music and dance's relationship with drama could be complete without reference to the vast number of children's operas and cantatas which have been written during the last ten to twelve years. As a composer of international fame, the late Benjamin Britten made a unique contribution to this area of musical activity from his 'Noyes Fludde' and 'St. Nicholas' to the 'Golden Vanity' and 'The Children's Crusade'. Composers such as Alan Bush, Hugo Cole, Richard Rodney Bennett, Gordon Crosse and Kenneth Platts have also featured prominently. Innovatory too are the jazz and pop cantatas composed by Herbert Chappell and the 'instant' operas of Malcolm Williamson, designed to be rehearsed and performed with the minimum of props in two hours or so. Unlike the once familiar Gilbert and Sullivan school production, children's opera is written within the technical and artistic abilities of the intended performers and, as a result, the word 'amateur' has become an anachronism in this context.

Perhaps the most widely-known and performed dramatic work for children (later made into a full-scale musical show for professional performance) is 'Joseph and the Amazing Technicolour Dreamcoat'. Composed by Andrew Lloyd Webber to a libretto by Tim Rice, this work shows a skilful blending of several popular musical styles and idioms. The original twenty-minute version which was written for a London boys' school permits maximum flexibility in treatment in accordance with a school's resources and rehearsal time. Apart from this, another reason for its tremendous popularity may be the fact that the full-length version is performed professionally by adults. It appeals to children and adults alike. Besides its obvious musical merits, it may well be that 'Joseph's' success is also due to the fact that it is not solely a work for children but designed for performers of any age and is set well within their musical capabilities.

Integrational possibilities

Integrative work has long been established in primary educational practice where 'project', 'topic' and 'thematic' approaches are widely used. Sybil Marshall's highly descriptive accounts of her educational methods (1963 and 1968) have shown that the thematic approach can be relevant to all stages of the curriculum and, if applied to teacher education, might well produce 'cultured' rather than merely 'trained' teachers.

The value of such work in the secondary school has been relatively unexplored, in all probability because of the over-riding importance attached to examination successes and essential syllabus coverage. A study made of music's use as an integrative element revealed that it was a rare occurrence (Schools Council 1972). This bulletin describes various experiments which have taken place in the secondary school curriculum. These have included a project where team teaching was also reinforced by set class periods of music; a project on African culture where more than 100 pupils were divided into five groups headed by teachers of literature, theatre, art, music and craft; and a curriculum development project where local authorities in the north-west collaborated with the Schools Council to integrate art, music, drama, physical education, English, science and mathematics.

Conclusions were difficult to draw from such a small sample of integrated schemes. Observations were made however that there appeared to be a noticeable improvement in pupils' attitudes to work, as well as evidence of improved co-operation with the teaching staff. It was also found that the framework of integrated studies could be of real benefit to musical pupils, providing additional stimulus to improvisation and composition. It was felt that, for the pupils, the main value of integrating music with other subjects was to show its relevance and to improve social attitudes. For the teacher it helped to dispel isolation and give a broader view of his own art. Here, there was an educative element as the schemes involved preparation, research and discussion with fellow members of the team. A possible reason why music as an integrator has been neglected up to now is that a bias towards performance largely conditions the attitudes of specialist teachers. The widely divergent training of music teachers may be another explanatory factor.

Paynter and Ashton are pioneers of the 'integrative' arts approach in secondary schools and have provided model lessons and suggestions for such work (Paynter and Ashton 1970). Their projects include, for example, 'Music and Words', 'Music and Drama', 'Movement and Music', 'Patterns in Nature', and 'Theatre Piece'. Guidance is provided on ways in which this type of thematic approach can be developed. On the value of integration to music Paynter and Ashton (1970, p. 19) point out that:

> Music suffers from isolation in the curriculum: it has for so long been regarded as a highly specialized subject. In fact it needs the other arts as much as they need it. If a team of teachers (art, movement, drama, English, music) work together with a class on one project, each will enrich the others.

Slade discovered that drama had a cathartic value for emotionally disturbed and delinquent youth who were able to work off their frustrations and aggressions through dramatic work. Advocates of the Paynter and Ashton approach might well substitute the word music or arts for 'child drama' in the following statement (Slade 1954, p. 119).

> One of the most important reasons for developing child drama in schools generally is not actually a therapeutic one, *but the ever more constructive one of prevention.* Prevention of many things is provided by the general balancing process, discovery of personal rhythm, and by 'playing out'.

More recently, Slade (1968) has focused on spontaneity as a dynamic phenomenon in human nature expressed in words, dance and music. He believes that spontaneous play is a natural therapy and that guided spontaneity is useful for all learning and general attitudes to life. Slade states that 'the expressive arts provide an enrichment to the total personality of the individual' (Slade 1968, p. 288), yet in attempting to convince the wider public of their value, it is often necessary to adopt a more scientific approach to their function. Slade has stressed that much more attention should be focused on the nature of young people and on what the arts might do for personal development when well taught. As a consequence of these views Slade's theory of play considers two types of human activity.

1 Projected activity — the passive form of activity which infuses the mind into object, symbols, cyphers, outside itself and brings them to life. This is seen in organization, government of others, the three Rs, crafts, painting and technical accomplishments.

2 Personal activity — the active form of activity where a human being takes on personal responsibility for doing something, being someone,

indulging in accurate communication, using the whole body in an active, physical sense, discovered in acting and in dance.

Paynter, Ashton and Slade have drawn attention to the potential of co-operative and integrative arts teaching. To publicize and generate more interest in this area there would appear to be considerable benefits from launching an 'Association for the Expressive Arts in Education'. Such an organization could strengthen the status of the arts in the curriculum and would establish realistic contact between the various teaching specialists. If evidence shows that appropriate integration of the arts serves to intensify the learning experience and provide a form of subliminal education, then this type of organization might well prove the major force which could convince educational authorities and institutions of their wider value.

Chapter 5
Monitoring achievement

Between the idea and the reality, between the motion and the act falls the shadow.

T.S. ELIOT, *The Hollow Men*

Music in the examination structure

General Certificate of Education (GCE) and
Certificate of Secondary Education (CSE)

For many years the traditional GCE examination in music was one which tested the following elements: melody writing; harmony; counterpoint; history of music with prescribed works; practical work in the form of dictation, aural and sight-singing tests; and some demonstration of instrumental skill according to the particular examining body.

In discussing the role of GCE examinations in the school music curriculum, Johnson (1968) expressed concern that, at Ordinary ('O') level too much emphasis was placed on the knowledge of the rudiments of music at the expense of practical work. An academic approach to harmony exercises often tended to emphasize the avoidance of faults at the expense of freedom of expression. The History of Music paper too was criticized for its encouragement of biographical details rather than a more analytical knowledge of specific musical compositions.

In recent years, however, the syllabus has undergone certain changes in which more freedom of choice is available at each level and, as in degree courses, opportunities now exist to weight examinations in the direction of an individual's interests and specific musical talents. The Northern Universities' Joint Matriculation Board (NUJMB) for example has, within the last ten years, introduced alternative syllabuses at 'O' and 'A' levels wherein syllabus A gives greater emphasis to academic study and syllabus B to practical ability, i.e. performance. Setting out its objectives at 'A' level the Board states

> A primary objective is to provide syllabuses which will enable teachers to plan stimulating and rewarding courses which give scope for individual interests and aptitudes.

In addition to music 'O' and 'A' levels there is an examination in the history and appreciation of music at 'O' level. This makes provision for pupils with more general interests than those wishing to study music beyond 'A' level.

The Associated Examining Board in its 'O' level examination acknowledges present day influences in its simple harmonization test. Here candidates are required to provide guitar chords as an accompaniment to a song in popular or folk idiom. In addition to the usual sight-singing and dictation tests, the practical tests include instrumental performance and the *viva voce* examination of a project file containing evidence of compositional skill or other special interests. At 'A' level this file takes the shape of a lecture file, consisting of three lectures prepared on a candidate's own choice of topic.

Aural tests in the 'A' level examination of the Oxford and Cambridge Board have also undergone a transformation. Melodic dictation is now presented on an orchestral instrument with simple piano accompaniment and two-part dictation on two different instruments. The departure from an almost universal use of the piano for administering aural tests is further emphasized by extracts performed by instrumental ensembles to examine recognition of instrumental timbres and special effects, and mistakes of notation and expression. The revision of this particular syllabus which now offers considerable freedom of choice is demonstrated by comparing the 1974 and 1978 'A' level syllabuses.

1974
Aural Tests
    Paper 1   Counterpoint and Harmony
    Paper 2   History of Music
    Paper 3   Analysis and Criticism
    Practical Examination   Grade VI of the Associated Board of the Royal Schools of Music

With the exception of Paper 3, the Special Paper, all the other sections of the examination were compulsory.

1978
  Section A (compulsory)   Aural Tests (Paper 1)
  Section B   (two items to be chosen)
    Outline of Western Musical History from 1550 to present day (Paper 2)
    Set Works and Musical Analysis (Paper 3)
    Techniques of Composition (Paper 4)
    Practical Examination

  Section C   (one item to be chosen)
    Essay
    Composition
    General Musicianship
    Additional Practical
    Further Subject of Merit or Interest

From the foregoing it is clear that not only is there more choice within the syllabus but also ample opportunity for candidates to display executant skills. For example, they could choose to take the practical examination in Section B on their first instrument plus either the additional practical in Section C on a second instrument or the general musicianship test should a second instrument prove to be not up to the required standard (a minimum of Grade VI standard is required for second study and Grade VIII for first).

Harmony and counterpoint are no longer compulsory requisites for study at 'O' level. The Oxford Delegacy enables candidates to submit the practical examination of the Associated Board (minimum Grade V) in lieu of Paper 2: Theory with Optional Harmony. Like the NUJMB, an alternative 'O' level syllabus was introduced in 1969 to provide for candidates with less specialized musical interests. Two factors which may have contributed to the demotion of harmony and counterpoint from their hitherto unassailable place in the GCE examination may be: the Certificate of Secondary Education (CSE) in which harmony and counterpoint exercises are practically non-existent (Long 1974); and the increasing importance being attached to practical performance examinations at school and university level. However a precedent already did exist in the syllabus of the University of Cambridge Local Examinations Syndicate in whose 'O' level, even before 1965, candidates could choose between the three alternatives harmony, general musical knowledge or practical examination.

At 'A' level evidence of greater freedom from constriction is seen in title changes such as the University of London's 'Harmony and Free Counterpoint' paper, which, in 1971 became 'General Musicianship'. The shift of emphasis which is gradually taking place in the study of prescribed works and periods is shown by the same board's 'O' level Paper 3 which, in 1969, was changed from 'Musical History and Set Works' to 'Analysis, Set Works and History'. The relevance of using real music and of testing in context is evident in the examining of musical rudiments. Where formerly this was done by means of isolated exercises it is now achieved through the analysis of a standard work.

For several years the Incorporated Society of Musicians and certain music educators have been seriously concerned that the system whereby only a single music 'A' level is available militates against those who wish to study music at a higher level. The case for separated as opposed to alternative music syllabuses has been made by Patrick Forbes (undated) supporting his argument by quoting the many examples of separated 'O' and 'A' levels available in other areas of the curriculum. For example, for many years it has been possible to offer at the same sitting the following examination combinations: at 'O' level – domestic science (food), domestic science (clothing); elementary mathematics, pure mathematics with statistics; biology, rural biology; and at 'A' level – geography and geology; history, ancient history; mathematics, further mathematics.

As Forbes (ibid., p. 4): goes on to say

> Universities in many parts of the world have, for many years, awarded degrees in musical performance (with some historical

backing) and in recent years some English universities have begun, if not to follow them, at least to treat performance more seriously than hitherto. This is a welcome step because once the universities recognize performance as important they will themselves influence the various GCE boards and perhaps even the School Council itself.

At the time of writing, new examinations have been announced by the Associated Examining Board and the University of London which show a marked shift of emphasis towards performance. The Associated Examining Board is introducing a new 'O' level where practical performance will take 60 per cent of the total marks. Similarly, the University of London Board is introducing a set of five new 'A' level music syllabuses to take effect from June 1980. More relevantly, it will be possible to take the Practical Music Examination at the same sitting as Theoretical Music, at last making double 'A' levels in music a reality. No doubt other boards will quickly follow this example and, in recognizing the subject's diverse components bring music into line with other subjects and inevitably enhance its value as an examination subject.

1965 saw the introduction of a new examination, the Certificate of Secondary Education (CSE). Showing a distinct emphasis towards the practical elements of music, the CSE boards have demonstrated a flexible approach to change and innovation. Indeed the 'three mode' examination procedure as an alternative to GCE 'O' level has given unique opportunities for reciprocity between the schools and the boards on matters of curriculum content. Advised by the inspectorate, the new boards have pursued the following general aims: the stimulation of corporate music making as part of the examination; the testing of musical literacy through the kind of aural perception required in actual performance; the encouragement of a wider knowledge of musical literature rather than an unnecessarily detailed study of two or three set works; and the encouragement of individual interests (Schools Council 1966).

A typical CSE examination format is that of the East Midlands Regional Board which is divided into three parts: A – musical literacy (individual reading and listening); B – musical knowledge (examined both aurally and by written work); and C – individual interest shown by means of a 'folio' giving details of musical performance, original composition, harmony exercises, individual subjects of study or a section of a class project.

Ensemble work is featured in the examination of the Welsh and East Anglian Boards although no mark is allocated for this section. On the other hand, the Associated Lancashire Schools Board allocates 20 per cent of the total marks to ensemble work on the basis of a continuing five year course assessment. The Practical Section which usually forms an alternative choice to the special study or individual interest examination is, in the majority of boards, awarded up to a third of the total mark allocation. Generally a strong feature of the examination in some cases (e.g. the Metropolitan and Southern Regional Boards), it carries an allocation of 35 per cent. The range of choice available in the special study or individual interest examination covers such topics as original composition, annotated programmes, or the making and playing of a simple instrument. The South–East Regional Board extends its suggestions to that of showing evidence of ability in conducting a group of younger pupils in singing, recorder playing or instrumental ensemble. This may be presented in the form of a concert or tape recording.

Multi-part questions requiring short responses are a strong feature of the South Western Board as opposed to the more conventional essay type of question. One paper on twentieth-century music asks questions requiring fifty to sixty short responses and this type of answer is required in the testing of musical literacy as well as knowledge of prescribed works.

The syllabus of the Metropolitan Board gives a choice of two special topics in addition to the study of a family of instruments. The wide range of options includes jazz and popular music as well as the more conventional opera, symphony, chamber music etc. Teachers' guidance notes are supplied for the study of 'popular music since 1950' with suggestions for studying current musical enthusiasms, identifying both the musical characteristics and the social influences connected with the groups concerned, and for tracing the origins of their styles back to the 50s and 60s (Attwood 1975). This initiative on the part of an examining board has led to an experiment in a London school where, under the 'mode 2' regulations an examination has been devised on popular music and where it is now possible to gain a CSE grade 1 pass in this specific subject (see Farmer 1977).

As can be seen from the writer's earlier work (Taylor 1977) there has been an appreciable rise in GCE and CSE music entries as a proportion of total arts examinations since 1965. Significant, too, has been the rise in passes at Grade I level in the CSE examinations during this period. Since 1966 the Schools Council has been working on various alternative examination structures to replace or reshape the present system. If such changes do take place, despite the opposition of universities and university examination boards (Walker 1976) the practical and innovatory endeavours of the CSE boards will undoubtedly be reflected in the structure of any new examination system. Most of all, they have attempted to devise means of examining the less readily evaluated areas of music, i.e. the practical day to day activities of the classroom music lesson. The 'group four' restraints proved extremely effective in devaluing music's place in the secondary school curriculum. Inevitably the CSE examination has helped to redress this situation by giving an academic seal of approval to the practical elements of music study which only examination status can provide.

External music examinations

No account of music examinations could be complete without some scrutiny of the external examinations of the Associated Board of the Royal Schools of Music (ABRSM) and the other London conservatoires. For almost a century standards in instrumental and vocal performance have been set by the graded examinations of these institutions. They have also been used to qualify candidates from exemption from the relevant practical sections of the GCE examinations since their inception.

In terms of subject entries the largest examination board is the ABRSM and Table 1 (p. 74) gives a detailed analysis of these examination entries over the period 1965–76. It is noteworthy that the total number of annual examined entries in Britain and Ireland has more than doubled over this period. Also evident is the dramatic rise in popularity of the guitar, brass and woodwind; the guitar being introduced into the syllabus by the ABRSM and the Trinity College in 1966. The London College of Music and the Guildhall School of Music and Drama also report increased interest both in the guitar and the recorder which was also introduced into their syllabuses comparatively recently. At the time of writing a new initiative has taken place, the creation of the London Percussion Examinations Board, which has just conducted its first examinations. Up until now, no academy, college, authority or board has set any graded percussion examinations yet, like the Associated Board, its standards may be soon accepted as part of 'O' and 'A' level practical requirements.

An interesting comparison can be made between the upsurge of interest in guitar, brass, woodwind and now percussion, with the fairly static numbers for piano, organ and singing since 1965. Entries for piano examinations have traditionally been of a numerical superiority yet it is clear that, as a percentage of total subject entries, the popularity of the piano has been in a steady decline for some time. Brocklehurst (1971) informs us that in 1946 piano entries formed 94 per cent of the ABRSM entries. From the available figures it is evident that by 1965 this had dropped to approximately 62 per cent, by 1970 to 55 per cent and by 1976, to 45 per cent.

Although it is reasonable to assume that nearly all candidates for these examinations are of school age, there is apparently a considerable entry from adults. The figures quoted also do not take into account the 62,000 overseas candidates who are examined each year all over the world (Cranmer 1975). The influence of these external examinations should not be underestimated. They are, as they have always been, easily available to the community as a whole. For both the amateur and the aspiring professional they still provide a challenging yardstick against which he can be measured from Grade I to Diploma level.

TABLE 1 Subject analysis for examinations of the Associated Board of the Royal Schools of Music from 1965–76 in Great Britain and Ireland.

	1965	1966	1967	1968	1969	1970	1971	1972	1973	1974	1975	1976
piano	72,732	76,436	78,372	80,631	87,530	92,653	101,868	101,295	105,418	102,141	105,229	110,994
organ	621	606	517	547	592	609	609	631	672	675	610	623
violin	9,468	9,868	9,705	10,787	13,965	15,434	16,544	18,947	21,808	24,022	24,539	26,473
viola	576	647	656	703	851	985	1,017	1,222	1,366	1,451	1,611	1,752
cello	1,689	1,991	2,145	2,431	2,936	3,533	3,713	4,497	4,845	4,969	5,704	6,523
double bass	107	127	140	166	173	202	253	322	239	273	370	388
guitar			67 first yr.	156	236	271	368	538	1,033	1,388	1,700	1,905
flute	961	1,253	1,442	1,867	2,375	2,962	3,459	4,353	4,463	5,442	6,542	7,904
oboe	460,	594,	745	936	1,088	1,346	1,404	1,846	2,128	2,385	2,596	2,913
clarinet	2,029	2,631	3,126	3,802	5,009	5,861	7,094	8,073	9,400	10,779	12,784	14,792
bassoon	74	100	118	180	226	285	345	419	549	574	594	711
horn	161	207	283	339	503	613	907	1,120	1,269	1,501	1,737	2,044
trumpet or cornet	412	522	740	1,019	1,344	1,826	2,210	2,709	3,260	3,594	4,491	5,378
trombone	142	147	199	280	509	661	832	1,049	1,194	1,390	1,679	2,123
other brass	22	34	70	78	647	944	1,025	1,350	1,812	2,182	2,885	3,531
harp	16	9	15	25	25	28	45	45	43	43	77	73
singing	1,833	1,654	1,892	1,922	2,237	2,450	2,203	2,271	2,428	2,504	2,399	2,446
musicianship	368	295	324	324	314	370	306	317	298	341	377	423
theory	25,529	25,579	27,675	28,543	31,583	33,602	35,628	41,961	43,276	45,687	50,032	53,406
piano duets	97	100	88	104	126	121	105	97	103	105	97	90
total examined	117,297	122,800	128,319	134,840	152,268	164,776	179,935	193,062	205,604	211,446	226,053	244,492

Source The Annual Reports of the Associated Board of the Royal Schools of Music 1965–76.

Advanced music education

Courses of advanced music education are provided in the main by four types of institution — colleges of education, universities, colleges of music (conservatoires) and polytechnics. During the last twelve years there have been many significant changes in higher education. Dramatic expansion has taken place in many institutions. Some smaller colleges have either been closed or have merged to form large units. Adult or 'lifelong' education has begun to take on new dimensions. The following pages are concerned with the main developments which have been taking place in music education at tertiary level. At the same time, specific reference is made to any factors which appear relevant to the teaching of music.

Colleges of Education

During the last decade colleges of education (known until 1963 as 'training' colleges) have undergone a concertina-like expansion and contraction. To meet the needs of increasing age cohorts, the number of teacher training places more than tripled from 32,464 in 1961 to 109,449 in 1971. In 1960 the certificate of education course was lengthened by a year to three years. This course was intensified and expanded to meet the ever increasing school population. It met its apogee in 1964–65 when the new Bachelor of Education degree was introduced, at which time there was the biggest outpouring of teachers since the war. The James Report (Department of Education and Science 1972c) gave support to the colleges in their aim to establish an all graduate entry into the teaching profession. This was to be implemented by gradually phasing out the three year certificate course and replacing it with BEd degrees of three (ordinary) and four (honours) years' length. In the same year the Government's White Paper *Education: a framework for expansion* announced plans to encourage colleges to develop either singly or jointly into major institutions of higher education and so remove them from their isolated roles as teacher training establishments (Department of Education and Science 1972a).

As a result of these policies many college mergers have taken place with neighbouring colleges of education, polytechnics and colleges of further education. At the present transitional state, the old certificate of education course is still being phased out and new bachelor degrees introduced, validated either by parent universities or the Council for National Academic Awards (CNAA). A student wishing to study music may now pursue a BEd degree in which, like the former certificate structure, there are three main components: main academic subject, the theory and practice of education and professional or curriculum studies. The syllabus is comprehensive but demanding for, in the space of three years, high standards must be reached in instrumental performance (usually including piano), practical composition, musical skills such as aural training, keyboard harmony and sight-singing, conducting, history and set works, musical pedagogy (including teaching practice), ensemble performance and direction, and special studies such as a miniature thesis or portfolio of compositions. Alternatively, entry may be made directly to a BA degree course, more akin to a conventional university course as at Newton Park College where a broadly based two-year music curriculum of composition, history and analysis, and general musicianship is followed by a third year of specialization in performance, composition etc. If the student then wishes to become a teacher it is necessary to obtain the appropriate professional teaching qualification by successfully completing a one year post-graduate course.

Interesting subject combinations have emerged including a joint honours BA at Loughborough College (now part of Loughborough University), where music can be combined with drama. A BEd degree in the performing arts is available at Madeley College of Education with concentration in music, drama with film, or dance. Movement studies with music, or dance with music, are new Bachelor of Humanities degrees offered at Nonington College of Physical Education. The latter is of particular interest for it has been the opinion of music educators that the omission of movement and dance study from advanced music education may have seriously hindered the development of music in schools (Renouf 1960). Isolated examples of music and movement as an interlinked study do exist as, for instance, in the Dalcroze Certificates courses run at Roehampton Institute of Higher Education but it may well be the influence of the new bachelor degrees in the creative arts and humanities and the initiatives of the Laban Art of Movement Centre which will eventually speed the acceptance of this naturally linked subject combination throughout higher education.

In addition to undergraduate courses some colleges provide one year postgraduate study for graduates of music conservatoires and university music departments. Often these courses are highly specialized, for example, dealing with the teaching of music to middle year children or for peripatetic instrumental teaching, as at Bulmershe College of Higher Education and the Manchester Institute of Higher Education. Courses of one term to one year are also available to seconded general teachers wishing to develop particular music skills or gain additional specialist teaching qualifications (see Jacobs 1976, pp 156–8). Both the Department of Education and Science and the Gulbenkian Foundation (Gulbenkian 1978) urge local authorities to concentrate on in-service training for class teachers, class music teachers and instrumental teachers. The need is seen, yet clearly the problem is one of finance. The Roehampton Institute of Higher Education (the institute resulting from the merger of the Froebel Institute College and Gypsy Hill College) has entered the postgraduate area with a taught MA in music education on the lines of the first degree of this kind established at London University's Institute of Education.

The years of expansion and development in higher education have been halted in part by the current economic recession. In the 1970s financial stringency has also coincided with a rapidly declining birth rate. In order to rationalize teacher provision many smaller colleges are either in the process of being, or already have been, phased out. The smaller intake and higher entrance requirements for college courses should lead to a system of greater selectivity and motivation. One could, therefore, reasonably forecast an improvement in music teaching standards. This would be particularly opportune in primary schools where music teaching has often been neglected, taught by non-specialist teachers or left to enthusiastic volunteers.

Stanley Hewett (1975, p. 4) pointed out that, in comparison with other careers, school teaching has for many years suffered from a lack of professional status. This has not been helped by the fact that the teacher in training has been isolated from his peer group. The new higher education structures which integrate professional teacher training alongside other forms of tertiary education should help to remedy this situation.

University departments of music

Student numbers at universities began to rise appreciably in 1946, expanded by a large proportion of ex-service men and women whose higher education had been disrupted by the war. 63,000 students entered universities in 1946–47 rising quickly to 85,421 by 1950 and increasing rapidly through the 1960s as a result of government expansion programmes designed to keep pace with the birth rate, the 'bulge' and rising aspirations. Not only was there a progressively increasing number of pupils staying on at school beyond the age of sixteen but also an accompanying increase in the number of university awards available from public funds (Dent 1961).

However, the immediate post-war period showed no comparable expansion in music student numbers. The position in 1954 was one where the size of undergraduate music faculties varied from as little as three to as many as 86 students. The number studying music as either a main or subsidiary study at this time in 15 universities and university colleges was only 429 out of a total number of 19,945 arts undergraduates, approximately one in every 46 (Long 1959). This proportion remained constant for many years for in 1965 the 655 music students represented only one in every 45 arts students (Department of Education and Science 1967).

For university music the important development of this period was the introduction of honours degrees at more than half of the English universities (see Table 2). As a result, music slowly built up its academic reputation and became an established university degree subject.

Beneficial as this recognition was in raising the status of music in the university curriculum, less fortunate was the resultant reinforcing effect which it had on an already narrow and constricted syllabus. Criticism

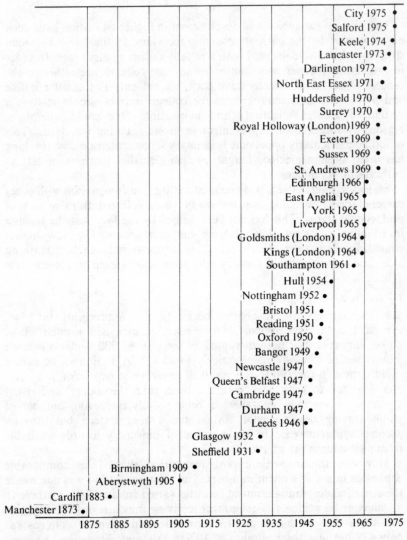

City 1975 •
Salford 1975 •
Keele 1974 •
Lancaster 1973 •
Darlington 1972 •
North East Essex 1971 •
Huddersfield 1970 •
Surrey 1970 •
Royal Holloway (London) 1969 •
Exeter 1969 •
Sussex 1969 •
St. Andrews 1969 •
Edinburgh 1966 •
East Anglia 1965 •
York 1965 •
Liverpool 1965 •
Goldsmiths (London) 1964 •
Kings (London) 1964 •
Southampton 1961 •
Hull 1954 •
Nottingham 1952 •
Bristol 1951 •
Reading 1951 •
Oxford 1950 •
Bangor 1949 •
Newcastle 1947 •
Queen's Belfast 1947 •
Cambridge 1947 •
Durham 1947 •
Leeds 1946 •
Glasgow 1932 •
Sheffield 1931 •
Birmingham 1909 •
Aberystwyth 1905 •
Cardiff 1883 •
Manchester 1873 •

1875 1885 1895 1905 1915 1925 1935 1945 1955 1965 1975

TABLE 2   Dates of establishment for honours degrees in music in universities and polytechnics in Great Britain.

Source   Taylor, 1977

was levelled at the over emphasis given to the craft of pastiche musical composition and the intensive training given in techniques which had little practical application in schools (Long 1959). With the majority of music graduates entering the teaching profession, Long's concern with relevance would appear most appropriate at this time. A typical syllabus for the bachelor's degree of this period was modelled on the traditional Oxbridge pattern. This consisted primarily of study in harmony, counterpoint, fugue, composition, orchestration, history of music, set works, aural classes, some keyboard musicianship (score reading and figured bass) and elementary acoustics. With few exceptions it was expected that instrumental performance would be studied outside the university with a private teacher.

There was concern about the lack of provision made for future music teachers at undergraduate level. A similar vacuum existed at post-graduate level and caused general professional disquiet. Simpson (1963) states that in the year 1955–6 there were 47 music graduates following certificate of education courses in 11 different education departments. Not only was this a wasteful and inefficient use of resources but a third of these education departments provided no specific training in methods of particular relevance to music teaching. The Standing Conference of Music Committees (1954), aware of these deficiencies, urged university education departments to pay particular attention to music training in order to encourage amateur musicians at the post-graduate stage to learn how to teach music as a subsidiary subject.

However, attempts to remedy this situation were being made, for by 1953 a specialized course had been established at Reading's Department of Education where specific training in music teaching methods, organization and practical work could be obtained (Bentley 1953). A similar course was later established at the University of London's Institute of Education in 1959.

By the late 1960s the number of university music departments had almost doubled yet it was still a point of some concern that the traditionally narrow degree curriculum should still be so generally followed by departments which offered little variation in course content though considerable variety in degree nomenclature (McCaldin 1968). For at Aberystwyth a BMus honours degree is of three years' duration whereas at Edinburgh it is three years for a general degree and four years for honours. At Cambridge, Leeds, Liverpool, Reading and Southampton the BMus is a postgraduate one year course taken after a BA degree, while at Durham and London it is an external degree.

Nevertheless innovation and change have taken place. With the exception of the early prototype, Keele, the establishment of new universities from 1961 onwards has been a key factor in the broadening of the university music syllabus and in the variety of subject combinations now available. As state foundations they have enjoyed a singular advantage of being free to innovate, to grant their own degrees from the very beginning and so plan their own curricula and methods of assessment. As Lord Annan states (Annan 1975, p. 26):

... the new universities built bridges between arts and sciences ...

and emphasised that knowledge had a social context and learning was not to be divorced from the needs of society.

Combining music with another subject for a joint honours degree is by no means innovatory. Instead it is the wider choice of subject combinations and their inter-relationship which typifies new university courses as shown in the following examples. York University's music department dates from 1965 when, as an alternative to the normal music degree, it pioneered and established a music and education degree combination. This was soon followed with other combinations such as music and theatre, and music with mathematics. The vocational bias of the music/education degree course is demonstrated by the inclusion of the following topics: the methods of Orff and Kodály; primitive music; music and drama; blues, pop and jazz; singing; voice production; guitar tuition. The early establishment of this concurrent degree has resulted in an expanding post-graduate research programme in music education and the basing at York of a School Council research project into music in the secondary school curriculum. Interesting also is the adoption of a teaching method more usually associated with primary education, that of vertically streamed project work. Students and post-graduates from any year may contribute to a chosen four week project in which each contributes his main strengths and expertise. Assessment is continual and the project folio remains open to enable a student to add to the work at subsequent times throughout the course. Considerable emphasis is placed on practical work and performance in a department where most of the staff are composers.

Keele's music department became fully established in 1974. As at York the course emphasis is on practical musical activity with traditional academic study as a basis and offers during the final year a choice of special studies such as performance or composition. A wide variety of subject combinations is possible – Music/Education, Music/Computer Science and Music/American Studies are but three examples. Departmental strengths and interests enable the joint Music/American Studies degree to be particularly integrative and already post-graduate courses in American music and popular music are underway. The installation of an electronic studio, familiar in tertiary education, has received a boost by the establishment of a research fellowship funded by the Leverhulme Trust.

Music is studied in a contextual pattern at Sussex University where a student has the choice of studying music within either the School of English and American Studies or in the School of Cultural and Community Studies. In the former, for example, a typical course might be 'Music and the American Society', in the latter, 'The Artist and the Public in Contemporary Society'.

A trend towards developing particular departmental strengths is already evident. At Lancaster, where a major course in music began in

1973, departmental emphasis is on study through performance. Here, instrumental tuition can amount to a third of the final degree assessment. At Glasgow, the bias is on composition, and at Hull on orchestral and choral conducting. Birmingham specializes in opera studies and stagecraft whereas Cambridge emphasizes the importance of paleography in its degree courses.

Instrumental performance as an integral part of the university degree curriculum is now generally emphasized. It has become increasingly common for performing artists to be invited to be 'in residence', often on long term appointments. The practice of having a resident string quartet appears to be the most common with piano quintets, string trios, numerous soloists, composers and conductors, completing a picture of practical and professional music making which has gathered momentum during the last ten to fifteen years.

The almost general acquisition of electronic music studios regenerates and reflects an interest in the scientific and mathematical aspects of music and the desire to provide resources for modern compositional techniques derived from 'musique concrete'. A unique BMus Tonmeister degree, available at Surrey University, prepares graduates for a career in the recording industry. BSc degrees are offered at Leeds (computational science and music), Salford (where music can be studied in combination with two scientific subjects), Keele (music and electronics, music with mathematics, music and physics) and the City University. The City's music course is interestingly a single honours BSc. Designed to fuse the elements of music both as an art and a science it may be a three year full-time or four-year sandwich course where a year in practical training is taken between the second and third years. The novelty of approach can be seen from the syllabus content: the literate sound world (survey of notations, analysis of western and eastern theories of instruments, the study of music as vertical and horizontal structures in sound); the non-literate sound world (musical anthropology, aural and rhythmic analysis of musical cultures); instrumental or vocal training (principal and second studies, basic aural training, conducting); the physics of sound; the biological and physiological aspects of sound; and the use of electronics in sound creation. All these areas are linked by studies in the psychological, philosophical and mathematical approaches to music. The third year syllabus offers specialization in any of the following areas: electronic and computer generation of sound; acoustics; sound engineering; music administration; music therapy; performance; editing and paleography; ethnomusicology, etc.

Since 1968 the traditional syllabus of the older civic universities has steadily changed to one which gives a broadly based two-year curriculum followed by a third year which allows choice of specialization in those areas in which the student's interests and greater abilities lie. For example, the BMus course at Sheffield University gives third year students the opportunity to weight the course by choosing two of the following options: performance (culminating in a diploma standard recital); composition through submitting a portfolio; or history of music where a thesis is eventually submitted on a specific area of study. A second series of options can weight these choices still further: ensemble class; analysis of twentieth-century scores; editorial techniques; acoustics; Italian or German language; music and television. For the BA dual degree at Sheffield a dissertation which specifically relates the inter-disciplinary aspects of both subjects is a third year requirement. In particular, the dual school of English and Music is so designed to cover those areas of study in which literature and music interlink, as, for example, in English folk song and television opera. There is today a greater career choice for music graduates than ever before. The course developments, which have been described, now lead to careers in music publishing, arts administration, musical journalism, the BBC and ITV and the recording industry, in addition to teaching and performance.

In common with other subject areas in higher education, post-graduate taught courses have been introduced leading to the qualifications of MMus, MA or Diploma in Music. At the University of London an MMus (one year) is available in four different study areas – musicology, composition, musical analysis or folk music. Two from four options are chosen at East Anglia for the MMus degree which offers the recording and production of music, composition, performance and musicology. The MA or Diploma in Music at Nottingham is a course on the interpretation and editing of renaissance and baroque music. The way in which universities can capitalize on departmental strengths is shown in a course providing training in the basic techniques and methods needed for research into early music as well as a scholarly training for performers specializing in this area.

Although these general developments have been prolific and healthily diverse, it is difficult to understand why courses on musical pedagogy have been so neglected. For, in sharp contrast, courses on music in education are few and far between. York and Keele's dual music with education combination have been described. In addition, four other universities provide an optional course in the second or third year. These are Lancaster's 'Music in Education' option, East Anglia's one term course option on 'Creative Experiment in School Music' for second and third year students, Royal Holloway's 'Music and Education' and Sussex's special subject 'Improvisation and Creative Work with Children's Groups'. It is significant that so few universities appear to offer any undergraduate course specifically relevant to school music and current classroom practice. Interestingly, with one exception, they are all new university departments.

The first taught Master's degree in music education has been introduced at the Institute of Education, University of London. All students study the psychology of music, aesthetics and social factors bearing on music education, and choose two areas for specialization from the following: practical work, the music curriculum and research methods in music education. The Institute's pioneering work in music education, as at Reading, has enabled its work to expand to MPhil and PhD research in various aspects of music education such as 'Music in Inner City Schools', 'Music and Creativity' and 'Music and the Adolescent'. Similarly, at Reading, the earlier work of Arnold Bentley has led to considerable postgraduate research into the differing aspects of musical ability and, in 1970, to the basing here of a Schools Council Research Project into the music education of young children.

The most recent figures available on student numbers indicate that from 1965 to 1973 there was a dramatic increase in the proportion of full-time students studying music (see Table 3).

TABLE 3 Proportional representation of music undergraduates in total 'arts' undergraduate university admissions.

undergraduates studying music as full-time study (main or subsidiary)		total number of arts undergraduates	proportion music:arts
Year	Number		
1954	429	19,945	1 in 46
1965	655	29,515	1 in 45
1973	1,278	43,606	1 in 34

Source Department of Education and Science 1975

In its fourteenth report (UCCA 1976) the University Central Council for Admissions indicates that this trend is continuing. Out of a total of 16,868 admitted to arts degrees in October 1976 the number admitted to university music degrees was 593, a proportion of 1 in every 28. As Table 2 shows, at least 15 honours degree courses in music have been established since 1965. Degree student numbers for music have increased accordingly, giving music a more prominent place in the arts faculties and undoubtedly making up for many years of stultification.

It is apparent that the narrowly academic degree syllabus of the 1950s has been transformed in the last decade to one which is not only more diverse but in many ways more related to other disciplines. In some of the newer departments a profusion of course options suggests that there may now be a danger of too much diversification where a student might graduate as a 'jack of all trades and master of none'. However, financial constraints may prove to be the stabilizing factor in achieving a necessary balance between the changeless need to master musical craftsmanship and the two increasingly important elements in university music study today — specialization in specific branches of music, and its application to and inter-relationship with other areas of study.

Colleges of music (the conservatoires)

From their early foundation the nine national music colleges have been primarily concerned with the training of the musician as a performer and as an instrumental or singing teacher. Therefore there is a deliberate emphasis within the standard three year course on individual tuition related to first and second instrument studies. A strong vocational bias to the college curriculum is reflected in the courses on the art of teaching which applies to the teaching of instrument or voice on an individual basis and is usually not orientated towards musical pedagogy in the wider sense. Exceptions to this are the Licentiate Diploma in School Music offered by the London College of Music, the Diploma in Musical Education at the Royal Scottish Academy of Music, and the Welsh College of Music's 'Music in Education' Course. However, prior to 1956, this was clearly not always the case, for Long (1959) has described how in the early post-war period it was quite common for classes in musical pedagogy to form part of the curriculum in the third year for students who had successfully completed what was then a normal two year course.

Although there is no ambiguity about the graduate qualifications of the colleges, e.g. GRAM, GBSM, GRNCM (Graduate of the Royal Academy, Birmingham School of Music, Royal Northern College of Music), there is a proliferation of nomenclature in other diploma courses whereby distinctions between associateships and licentiateships, internal and external diplomas become equivocal and confusing (see Gulbenkian 1965). If the recommendations of the recent follow-up report (Gulbenkian 1978) were to be implemented many of these ambiguities could be cleared up. For the Gulbenkian Committee advocate that the music colleges should adopt a two-year Dip HE course followed by two years to a degree with the flexibility of being able to transfer to or from a university or college of higher education.

The Standing Conference of Music Committees, concerned with the training of music teachers (Standing Conference of Music Committees 1954) felt that more provision could be made for class music teacher training in training colleges or university departments of education which were financially and practically better equipped than the conservatoires for this work. Accordingly this trend was followed although it was not until 1973 that a post-graduate certificate of education became obligatory for music college graduates wishing to be class teachers in state schools. The recent Gulbenkian Report also supports this earlier recommendation, suggesting that the conservatoires should concentrate on training performers and instrumental teachers and that class teacher training should be confined to the Trinity College. Yet there is a strong argument for resisting what appears to be a retrograde step. Many music college graduates are employed as peripatetic teachers with local education authorities. The group teaching system in which they find themselves is very different from the more traditional one–to–one teaching situation, and one which requires an appreciation of general educational practice as well as class music teaching skills. An extremely subject orientated training could not claim to give an adequate preparation for the school environment.

The Standing Conference stated that the music college's primary function is to train musicians. This could not be disputed, yet we are apparently training too many would-be professional musicians (Gulbenkian 1978). One could realistically assume that the supply of performing artists will always outstrip demand. Most graduates will be engaged in either part-time or full-time teaching at some stage of their life. Consequently it would be more practical to support programmes of concurrent training in which the aim is to foster the dual 'artist–teacher' combination. This quality is nowhere more exemplified than in Yehudi Menuhin who successfully combines a performing career with the educational interests of young musicians in his specialist school and his scheme for giving them performing opportunities (i.e. the 'Live Music Now' scheme). If such a course were adopted then the tendency to judge music college trained teachers as 'failed' or 'second class' performers would quickly be eradicated.

Clearly certain innovations have appeared in the curriculum of music colleges in recent years. The scope of instrumental training has widened to include the study of instruments such as the lute, saxophone, tuba and guitar. The increasingly general interest in mediaeval and renaissance music is shown in the growth of the number of optional courses appearing. Jazz is now featured in the syllabus and further developments are discernible in the extended range of options such as Indian music, composition for film, TV and radio, paleography, ethnomusicology and, of direct relevance to music teaching, the psychology of music. For many years the Royal Northern College of Music has run a joint course with the University of Manchester's music department. The opportunity to study for a London University degree exists at the Royal Academy, Royal College and the Trinity College. Recently a joint course has been organized between the Guildhall School of Music and Drama and the music department at the City University. An interesting development at the Guildhall School is the post-graduate diploma in Music Therapy, a pioneering course in this field.

Two final points stand out with respect to the music colleges. First, students may enter a graduate diploma course on the strength of five 'O' level GCE passes and evidence of superior performing ability. Other diploma courses may be pursued without these 'O' level qualifications if performing ability is of a particularly high standard. If, like other institutions of higher education, colleges of music were to introduce their own degrees, entry requirements would have to be raised to conform with other higher educational establishments. Second, in the light of developments taking place in the syllabuses of the examining boards, performance is steadily gaining respectability as an academic qualification and carrying increasing weight in the 'O' and 'A' level syllabus. As the first conservatoire to become part of an institution of higher education is the Birmingham School of Music (incorporated by the Birmingham Polytechnic in 1970) it will be interesting to see if it will become the first conservatory to introduce a CNAA degree course with a strong performing orientation. If present trends continue it is not difficult to imagine performance degrees, rather than diplomas, becoming the norm. Certainly North American experience would appear to support this view.

Polytechnics

The music centres established in technical colleges, colleges of further education and polytechnics have already been described. From these beginnings strong music departments have taken root to provide foundation, diploma and degree courses for students from the age of 16 to 21 and over. The opportunity to prepare 16 to 19-year-old students with the necessary basic skills prior to pursuing a main course of study in the *same* institution, music college or university must be unique. One such music department is that of Huddersfield Polytechnic, which, in 1965, had an enrolment of approximately 100 students under 19 years of age following a foundation course leading to 'A' level music and practical performance qualifications. In addition there were approximately 35 students studying for the two year diploma in music. By 1975 the range of courses had been extended to include the foundation course, external diplomas (ARCMs etc.), two to three year diploma in music, three year BA (Hons) (CNAA) and MPhil degrees.

The two or three-year diploma or certificate courses run by polytechnic schools of music are designed primarily with class music or school instrumental teachers in mind and accordingly are often divided into two categories. Apart from the compulsory classes on history, composition and aural training, instruction is given in voice and choral technique and importance is attached to the development of keyboard skills. Instrumental lessons and practice on first and second studies are given strong emphasis. In addition, group instruction is given on, for example, useful classroom instruments such as the guitar and recorder. At Huddersfield satisfactory participation in departmental activities such as the orchestra, choir, chamber music, accompanying and conducting contributes to the final diploma assessment. The curriculum of the Colchester Institute includes music of the twentieth century in concert hall and classroom, the application of new ideas in education, practice teaching, and projects concerning the teaching of music or on compositions suitable for school use.

The first CNAA honours degrees in music were initiated at Huddersfield (1970), at the Colchester Institute (then the North-East Essex Technical College and School of Art) (1971) and at Dartington

College of Arts (1972). The philosophy behind these degrees is basically that of considering three elements to be of equal importance: performance, composition, history and analysis. In addition, a number of options is offered which allow for limited specialization. High performance standards are facilitated by the number of professional performers on the teaching staff and, unlike some university music departments, a large music student body enables orchestral and choral practices to be a 'timetabled' rather than an extra-mural activity.

The BA syllabus at Huddersfield gives equal emphasis during the first and second years to performance (two instruments), composition and the history of music. In the third year, one of these subjects is dropped in order that the other two studies may be pursued in greater depth. In the first two years tuition is also given in orchestration, general musicianship and voice training; in the third year, analysis and interpretation. Throughout the course optional classes in choral and orchestral conducting are available.

At the Colchester Institute the BA syllabus is designed primarily to meet the needs of those intending to become teachers of music in schools and adult institutions. Music is viewed as an essentially practical study and the course aims to develop practical skills, at the same time providing the necessary academic background to support their development. This emphasis on practical work is shown in the second and third years where students choose one of four main subjects in which to specialize: performance; conducting and rehearsing; form; styles and textures; or composition.

The third institution, Dartington College of Arts, although unique in its inception, is included in this section as its degree course development has so closely followed that of the two polytechnic institutions. In keeping with its founding principles the degree course offered at Dartington gives special emphasis to twentieth century music and the study of music in various communities and cultures. In the second and third years the student may specialize in two areas chosen from: performance; composition; music in society (involving practical work in selected communities); and the music of India (which includes tuition on the sitar and tabla.

As might be expected, it is evident that the polytechnic institutions have developed degree courses with a strong practical emphasis. Such courses have a clear relevance for those who choose to teach in schools or for those intending to enter other distinct areas of the music profession. That there is also diversification between the three curricula briefly described is an additional indication of healthy growth and self-confident independence.

Adult or 'life-long' education in music

'Life-long' education is a term which may be used to describe all learning opportunities for adults taken up after full-time schooling has ceased and usually after a period in employment. As a concept, life-long learning is by no means new. What is new, however, is today's conscious attempt to provide constant access to educational opportunities throughout life. The Russell Report (1973) drew attention to the educational needs of those outside the conventional undergraduate age span. The Open University has demonstrated, with marked success, innovative means of responding to these needs.

Music has a long and historical place in adult education. Hale (1947) devotes considerable space to recount the prominent work achieved in the 1930s by, for example, the Workers' Educational Association, university extral-mural departments, women's institutes and guilds, the YMCA and men's clubs. Interestingly, the first rural music school at Hitchin, was originally founded to serve the specific needs of adults (Ibberson 1978). All these initiatives, together with the work of Leonard Elmhirst and F. G. Thomas at Dartington Hall (Bonham-Carter 1958) stand as landmarks in adult music education.

Apart from isolated exceptions until fairly recently music in adult education almost exclusively tended to mean classes in musical appreciation, organized as gramophone recitals demanding little or no active student involvement. Recent developments reveal a varied range of courses with a marked trend towards those designed for maximum student involvement and participation at every level. Morley College and the City Literary Institute have a long standing tradition for part-time music courses and activities. These range from individual instrumental tuition and intensive coaching in aural work and analysis to university extension courses in harmony, counterpoint and musical history. Classes in country music are juxtaposed with jazz and rock. In addition to these weekly activities Saturday morning classes involve parents and children in 'Family Music Making', 'Family Choir' and 'Suzuki Violin Class'.

Goldsmiths' College, University of London admits people of all ages to degree courses in music and music and drama. The music department's close partnership with the School of Adult and Social Studies not only reinforces the strength of its recurrent education programme but also facilitates part-time and evening study. Both part-time and full-time students are able to pursue foundation level courses and degree courses leading to BMus, MMus, MPhil and PhD qualifications.

Typical one day in-service and short courses are those run on, for example, mediaeval music, jazz, percussion and steel band music in schools. There are regular monthly residential courses, often organized in collaboration with societies and associations. Appropriate to an adult education programme which concentrates on jazz and popular music is one such course on clarinet and saxophone repair and maintenance run co-jointly with the Clarinet and Saxophone Society.

Nene College, Northampton, is part of the University of Leicester's Department of Adult Studies and draws students from as far as 30 miles away. Here a strong and increasing demand for practical, active courses is being met in several ways. 'Musical Appreciation' has become an active course involving background reading and listening, essay writing, discussion and aural training. By linking appreciation classes with the local concert season and by inviting composers to talk about their work, musical appreciation has become much more relevant to both student and tutor. A newer development is the musicianship course which is seen as the real 'nuts and bolts' of music provision, covering as it does the grammar and vocabulary of music with weekly homework and regular aural training sessions. This is extended to special aspects of musicianship such as basic harmony, contrapuntal techniques, the art of song writing and elementary composition. Replacing the more conventional 'sit-up-and-sing' type of choir are study choirs where the programme often includes more unusual works which, in addition to being rehearsed are also analysed and placed in historical perspective. All these courses are supplemented by lecture–recitals, music workshops, day schools and short-term residential courses.

In adult studies BBC radio plays a vital role. 'Music in Principle' is a typical series of programmes which deals with the concepts of melody, rhythm, mode, timbre, form etc. encountered in all types of music. 'Music Maestro Please' explores how music is produced by following the processes which a performer undergoes in order to recreate a composition. Again, this programme follows the new BBC philosophy of teaching music of all types by cutting right across conventional boundaries of style and genre.

As an innovator, the Open University is undoubtedly having a major impact on adult and recurrent education and giving the movement a much needed boost. Adoption of the American credit system ensures that individuals devise degree courses to suit their individual requirements. Music study is set within an interdisciplinary structure at foundation and second year level with specialist music courses at third and fourth year levels. The most recent development in the syllabus has been the 'Elements of Music' course which teaches basic harmony, aural training and analytical skills to beginners or near beginners. Students receive recorder tuition and each is loaned a four octave reed organ. The demand for this course is proving to be considerable not only as one studied for its own interest but as a prerequisite for the specialist third level courses. Music also forms part of an Associate Course on the Pre-School Child. Here course materials and a gramophone record are provided which enable the student to learn with the child many of the fundamental concepts of music and musical development.

The demand for Open University music units has already been high and the impact and spin-off effect seems likely to be very significant. The unique use of mixed media as a teaching tool – radio and television, gramophone records, correspondence tuition, personal contact, day and summer schools — brings a new sophistication to teaching techniques and methods. Some of these might be effectively employed in traditional teaching establishments. Open University students, as parents, will have an awareness of the organization and teaching methods of their own children's schools and, over time, should prove to be an influential pressure group for the maintenance of teaching standards and the quality and content of the curriculum.

The Open University is proving to be a practical way of giving people not just a second chance but multiple chances for education and qualifications. In turn, its graduates may well create a demand for higher degree courses and research facilities at their local universities and polytechnics. Other institutions are already emulating the Open University credit system and allowing credits to be transferred from one institution to another, be it college, university or polytechnic. This breaking down of traditional hierarchies should prove most beneficial to the interests of adult learners and lead to greater educational accessibility. Until now, to an alarming extent, many of our higher education institutions have turned their backs on the needs of the whole community. This is paradoxical when, for example, many universities originated as evening institutes set up by the populace which they served before becoming university colleges and finally independent universities.

The foregoing examples show the variety of music provision which is now available to the general public. A very useful guide to facilities and courses offered in the London area is provided by East (1978). Throughout the country, though widely dispersed and often, from necessity, fragmentary, adult music provision represents the 'tip of an iceberg' which has the potential to develop into a cohesive network of recurrent education opportunities for music education throughout life. For this to happen, there must be a national policy and will to facilitate first, incremental learning, to enable people to register for educational courses whenever relevant and practicable by means of a system of credit units and transferability; second, community involvement, following the example of American 'out-reach' programmes; and third, bearing both professional and leisure needs in mind, continuous education for both academic credit and pleasure.

Chapter 6
Counterbalancing forces

> Each step we make today toward material progress not only does not advance us towards the general well being, but shows us on the contrary, that all these technical improvements only increase our miseries.
>
> TOLSTOY

The preceding two chapters have been primarily concerned with the structure and content of the music curriculum at various levels. Clearly no teacher or educational system operates in a vacuum isolated from external influences. This chapter, therefore, describes some of the agencies which serve to promote and sustain music in education and musical activity generally. To put these influences into perspective various constraining factors, resulting from accelerated technological and social change, are then described.

Societies and associations

More than 100 associations and agencies are concerned with the needs of the music teaching profession or some aspect of music in education. The primary function of many of these bodies is to take care of particular interests such as salaries, fees and working conditions, or it may be to promote and safeguard the quality and quantity of musical provision both in the school and community.

The Incorporated Society of Musicians (ISM) is a large body representative of a wide spectrum of the music profession. In particular, the ISM's Music in Education section has lobbied for certain educational improvements. Its campaign for separated music examinations at 'A' level was conducted by making frequent representations to the relevant examining bodies and to the press. Another important issue seen by the ISM is the need for an organized effort from all interested groups to establish fundamental yardsticks for the primary music curriculum. It is felt that such action would be a positive and much needed step in alleviating those problems of transfer which regularly occur at secondary school entry. The ISM have also attempted to influence school authorities to timetable choral and instrumental music making during normal school hours. By tradition these activities have almost always been considered extra-curricular concerns.

Another body, the Standing Conference for Amateur Music (SCAM) is an association consisting of local authority music committees and national organizations primarily concerned with music education and amateur music making. The report which the Conference published on the Training of Music Teachers (SCAM 1954) is a notable publication in which the SCAM focused on specific educational needs. This association has also played an active role in sponsoring musical research, for example, the 'Music and the Slow Learner' project at Dartington, already described.

Earlier a description was given of the Rural Music Schools' Association's role in establishing music centres in relatively isolated areas of the country and in pioneering innovatory teaching methods. Like SCAM this association plays a useful part in disseminating information through courses, conferences and research findings, in addition to matters of general musical interest. Professional journals, in particular the *Music Teacher* and *Music in Education* provide a professional platform for voicing concern, testing opinion and lobbying for reform, apart from their function of informing music teachers of current trends and developments.

There are associations for promoting musical instruments, whose educational departments arrange courses for teachers at home and abroad. Other associations initiate and support youth bands and orchestras at local, regional and national level. In addition, there are societies and centres devoted to particular music educational methods such as the Dalcroze Society, the Orff-Schulwerk Society and the Cambridge Ward Method Centre. In all, there is a large number of organizations covering a wide spectrum of interests. Singly and co-operatively they are able to act as pressure groups for promoting music in and outside school.

Government reports and curriculum development

Government reports and curriculum development projects have served to draw attention to the status of school music with particular concern for the needs of the primary school. As Ross (1975) points out, all the major educational reports from Hadow (Board of Education 1926) to Newsom (Central Advisory Council for Education 1963) have stressed the need to raise the status of music and the arts in the school curriculum. Some of the Newsom Report's findings on secondary school provision have already been described. Similarly the Plowden Report (Ministry of Education 1967, para. 686) pointed out

> ... that progress was, and still is, very slow, mainly because of the neglect of systematic music instruction in the grammar schools and colleges of education and the consequent musical illiteracy of the great majority of teachers.

By pinpointing areas of concern these reports have drawn the teaching profession to look more closely at its work and take steps to initiate improvements. The Plowden Report underlined the weakness in continuity between primary and secondary school music (para. 687) and stressed how, as a creative subject, it lagged behind work in language and visual arts and crafts. The Newsom Report pointed out the major problem which beset the secondary school – inadequate resources, poor accommodation, a shortage of qualified teachers and a generally neglected status reflected by the poor regard in which it was held by many young people.

It was government reports such as these which brought attention to bear on many curriculum problems. In 1964 the establishment of the Schools Council for the Curriculum and Examinations represented a positive step towards making curriculum change and innovation a practical reality. Set up to 'find ways and organize means of reviewing and reforming the school curriculum' (Schools Council 1968*b*, p. 1) the Schools Council subsequently reinforced the findings of the Newsom Report in their own Enquiry 1 (Schools Council 1968*a*) and later in its working paper on music and the young school leaver (Schools Council 1971).

Enquiry 1 provoked action in the form of a four year curriculum study, 'The Arts and the Adolescent', which ran from 1968 to 1972. Directed by Ross and Witkin, the aim of this study (Ross 1975, p. 18) was

> ... to offer a rationale for the place of the arts in secondary education so as to assist teachers and others to discriminate between the aims which should receive particular emphasis in the building of a new curriculum.

This project, involving the active participation of thirty-six pilot schools revealed three factors detrimental to the arts curriculum (Ross 1975, p. 24).

a The set of traditional assumptions about the role of the arts in society and in education that push the work of artists and the work of arts teachers well down the list of social and educational priorities.

b The feeling that arts teachers are 'different' — often resulting from the more varied training background from which they came.

c The crossed purposes of the arts curricula today — the lack of a pervading concensus of goals and objectives.

Ross and Witkin set out to construct a basic conceptual framework for the arts teacher in response to what they saw as the general predicament of arts education: the confusion of the teacher as to his role and the educational function of his subject. This framework is presented in *The Intelligence of Feeling* (Witkin 1974). Here Witkin maintains that the prime concern of the arts curriculum should be the child's emotional development through creative self-expression, and that teachers who value subjective experience could be assisted in their curriculum planning by his analysis of the creative process through which the 'intelligence of feeling' is expressed.

After Ross and Witkin's study, two curriculum development projects on music education were initiated, one for secondary schools and the other dealing specifically with the education of young children. Like the project just described, 'Music in the Secondary School Curriculum' has been strongly influenced by the work of Suzanne Langer. It takes as its starting point the concept of artistic experience as an emotional one, namely a 'feeling' response. Begun in 1973 this five year project (funded with a £77,000 budget) is directed by John Paynter and Roy Cooper and based in the Department of Music at York University. The aim of 'Music and the Secondary School Curriculum' is to 'define and develop principles by which music may become a greater educational force in the secondary curriculum' (Paynter 1973). Its concern is not to find better ways of educating potential professional musicians but to examine the role of music in the total curriculum of the secondary school. As a consequence, the project team has set out to develop schemes and materials for classroom work which appear especially relevant to the emotional needs of young people. This essentially activity orientated project is based on classroom experimental work and draws on the expertise of a university department specializing in music education as well as from successful classroom practice (see Griffiths 1977). Materials and guides are field tested in approximately 200 participating schools. In addition there are courses, conferences and regular news-sheets which disseminate information, provoke feedback and serve to involve many educators in a co-operative learning venture.

It may well be that, on completion of this project, some long established views on the curriculum may be sacrificed while other aspects of music teaching traditions may be reinforced. Cooper (1974) states:

> It begins to look as if what is required is the discovery and definition of a whole new area of music teaching; perhaps many new areas the like of which we may not have experienced before and which will be suitable and work for the majority of our pupils who will never be touched by current teaching methods.

From an almost obsessive attention to the needs of the adolescent the other Schools Council Music Project has been rather different in orientation. Begun in 1970 'The Music Education of Young Children' (financed with a £90,730 grant) was completed in 1977 and may well have originated in response to the results of the Plowden enquiry. Directed by Dr Arnold Bentley and Ian Kendell at the University of Reading's School of Education, the purpose of this project was to discover how young children acquire musical learning, to clarify and define the aims of music education and to prepare materials to help teachers who are mainly non-specialists.

As at York this project was able to draw upon the research expertise of a university department. Its main task was the assembling and grading of existing music materials and the development and trial of new materials in forty pilot schools and nearly 100 associated schools. With an eventual goal of providing a structured core curriculum for use by non-specialists due regard was paid to maintaining an equal balance between the creative, recreative, listening and comprehensive elements of music. Like the early stages of a Language Development Programme, the materials have been designed to enable a child to work at his own rate in order to be ultimately musically independent (Kendell 1974). Creative work cards are intended to provide experience in handling notes in the way that speech precedes reading and writing. In the same way pre-readers are meant to foster some of the skills involved in music reading such as left to right orientation and the matching of sound with symbol. Musical concepts are encouraged through stories with accompanying tape recordings of sounds and activities and there are games to assist memory and visual and aural discrimination. Singing is seen to be fundamental to all music making. Recognizing that even in this activity individual rates of learning appertain, children are able to learn songs by rote from recorded examples. So that music can be seen as an integral part of everyday life there is positive encouragement to interrelate it to other classroom activities whenever relevant. Therefore the authors have provided materials which overlap with language development, mathematics, story and movement, and songs where the text relates to other areas of learning.

With the exception of the nursery school stage, this structured programme is now complete for the infant and junior stages and marketed by E. J. Arnold under the title *Time for Music*. The project has also led to the establishment of a permanent music centre at Reading University which, in addition to housing the project's materials, is intended to be a focal point for music education workshops, research programmes and in-service training courses.

The normal music curriculum has been an almost neglected sphere of educational research in terms of government backing. Therefore these two Schools Council projects represent long overdue initiatives and ones which may have a considerable impact on classroom practice.

Patronage and sponsorship

In promoting and sustaining music and the arts patronage now exists in many interesting forms. The traditional form of private patronage is still by no means uncommon, making a particularly valuable contribution to smaller arts ventures. There are also non-profit making foundations which fulfil an important function in complementing official sources of subsidy.

Foremost among these foundations is the UK branch of the Calouste Gulbenkian Foundation. Diggle (1975, p. 11) states that, in 1974, this body gave over £280,000 to the arts. In addition to its subsidizing activities the Calouste Gulbenkian Foundation has shown considerable concern for the education of the potential professional musician. Thirteen years after publishing its report *Making Musicians* (1965) the Foundation has now produced *Training Musicians* (Gulbenkian 1978). This follow-up enquiry makes recommendations for the improvement of training for musicians at all levels. Some of the Report's more controversial suggestions have already been described. Other main recommendations are:

1 The early identification of musical talent in the primary school as a first priority.

2 Increased local authority provision for music, particularly for instrumental teaching in secondary schools.

3 The subsidizing by local authorities of tuition with private teachers and the drawing up of panels of approved teachers for music centres.

4 More widespread local authority support for children at specialist music schools.

It remains to be seen in the years to come whether the local authorities can be persuaded to provide the necessary finance to implement these recommendations.

Patronage in the form of subsidy from national sources has expanded considerably since the early initiatives of the Council for the Encouragement of Music and the Arts and particularly during the last decade. For the year 1965/66 the Arts Council budget was reported to have been just below £4 million, yet ten years later the sum had increased to over £26 million (Diggle 1975, p. 9). Even when making allowances for inflation this represents a quite considerable increase in public spending on the arts. The structure and administration of the Arts Council has also changed dramatically during the last ten years (see Redcliffe-Maud 1976). Devolution of power through regional organizations has created a more equitable distribution of financial resources. There are now fifteen regional arts associations in England and Wales financed mainly by the national body with supplementary funds from regional county councils. Additional support comes from organizations such as the Gulbenkian Foundation, from industry, district councils and from membership subscriptions.

One such regional association, the East Midlands Arts was founded in 1969 and currently receives an annual income of approximately £200,000. Of this sum about £70,000 is given as grant-in-aid to arts activities in a region comprising Leicestershire, Nottinghamshire, Northamptonshire, part of Derbyshire and the new city of Milton Keynes. Grants are also awarded to subsidize publications, to mount exhibitions and to purchase equipment. They are also given to bodies such as music clubs and to individuals in the form of fellowships.

Another important function of regional associations is to make the arts more widely accessible by making them mobile in the form of touring events. Tours are organized for various art forms, for example, small-scale opera, chamber music, jazz and contemporary music. The encouragement and development of young audiences is seen to be another vital function of regional associations. For this purpose the East Midlands Arts has now established an East Midlands branch of the Youth and Music Association. Originally a London organization, the Youth and Music scheme has been operating for twenty-four years and grew out of the Robert Mayer's Children's Concerts. Designed to give the 14 to 25-year-old age group the chance to hear professional opera, concert and ballet at concessionary prices it is only recently that Youth and Music has expanded into other areas of the country with centres at Manchester, Liverpool, Sheffield, Leeds, Sunderland, Newcastle, Southampton and Nottingham. Obviously this development is an essential step towards educating and building future adult audiences for cultural events.

Other regional developments in providing for the arts have taken place. Recently reorganized local authorities have created new departments of leisure services for recreation and the arts. Carrying out policies and practice in sympathy with the Regional Arts Associations, these local authority departments carry the devolutionary process a stage further by organizing and financing cultural events at county and district level. In this way they are helping to bring international artists to hitherto remote areas as part of a cultural public service.

'Patronage' has been defined (Diggle 1975, p. 9) as essentially 'an altruistic activity carried out with no expectations of return other than the satisfaction of knowing that good is being done'. Halfway between this form of support and commercial 'sponsorship' are the foundations established by companies such as the Granada and the Stuyvesant Foundations. With little or no demand for public acknowledgement or overt publicity these enterprises have provided and continue to provide considerable sums of money for music and the arts. In the first ten years of its life, for example, the Granada Foundation gave £218,413 to support artistic and cultural activities. The Stuyvesant Foundation, for its part, has supported the London Symphony Orchestra and the Glyndebourne Festival Opera for many years.

Commercial sponsorship, on the other hand, is considered to be an activity where a sponsoring company hopes to receive some immediate and direct benefit as a result of its financial outlay. Although sports sponsorship is by no means new, the sponsoring of music and the arts by industry and commerce is a comparatively recent trend and one which is developing rapidly. In terms of public relations, performances and exhibitions are events which involve large numbers of people and, as such, are a valuable means of improving the public's awareness of a company.

The most prominent sponsors of musical activities are the major banks, insurance companies, tobacco firms and wine merchants. Financial backing is currently benefiting a wide range of enterprises: national orchestras, opera companies, concerts and tours, festivals, conductor's awards, the commissioning of new works and the subsidizing of classical records. Commercial sponsorship has great benefits too for live audiences, for subsidy may effectively reduce the cost of seats. In this way cultural events are made financially accessible to a wider and potentially younger audience. The same effect may result from the subsidizing of classical record production to bring records in the 'budget' category. Sponsorship operates not only in favour of national enterprises but can work also to the advantage of activities in the regions where prominent sponsoring companies are located. In this respect Bristol is considered to be an exceptionally favoured city for there three major sponsoring companies are based.

Arts sponsorship is a fast developing movement which may soon be as familiar as the sponsoring of sports and athletic events. In a time of increasing costs, financial backing of this kind may prove the most effective means of complementing government, local authority and private funding and be of benefit to both sponsor and sponsored. In sum, two dramatic changes have taken place during the last decade with regard to patronage and sponsorship of music and the arts. One, the impact of devolution which has resulted in a more equitable distribution of resources over the country in terms of finance and accessibility. Two, the more recent development of commercial and industrial arts sponsorship as a major component in meeting heavy and constantly rising arts costs. The effect of these initiatives should help to create wider, potentially more appreciative and knowledgeable audiences, which in turn could raise standards generally and foster consumer demand for music tuition, greater provision and participation.

The rise of the leisure industry

It would appear that never before have cultural activities been so widely accessible as within the last decade. At the same time there has appeared a corresponding rise of a commercial leisure industry which at times competes with these cultural developments.

An interesting view of the origins of the leisure industry is given by Pickering (1968, chapter 4) in which he gives a vivid description of the nineteenth-century church as a place of entertainment. Referring to the socio-religious activities which were a common feature of the non-conformist church Pickering (1968, p. 90) states:

> It is not too much to suggest that, in the period of say 1870 to 1914 the chapels, certainly in the large towns, performed the function of providing entertainment for local people. Some might be so bold as to say that in some respects the chapels were the forerunners of the provincial theatres and cinemas.

As part of an inevitable social process technology was to introduce in the

1930s more attractive forms of mass entertainment, such as the cinema, radio and car. Subsequently, many chapels were converted to cinemas or public libraries. In due course cinema going was also to be superseded as a popular pastime by television viewing (although there has been some revitalization in recent years as large cinema structures have been converted into smaller units).

Some post-war aspects of cultural change with the impact of television, increased affluence and the 'bulge' have been briefly described. Golding (1974) provides an enlightening account of developments in the growth and power of the mass media in the last ten years. In terms of technological development a stage of communication has now been reached which promises 'localization' and 'internationalization' (Golding 1974, p. 105). The former has resulted from the introduction of BBC and commercial local radio stations coupled with experimentation with local (cable) television.

The ever increasing power of the mass media (publishing, film, radio, television, record and tape) results from the fact that they have passed through a process first of industrialization, then of concentration. As Golding (1974, p. 44) points out:

> In 1972 average weekly household expenditure on the media and entertainment was higher than on clothing or household durables. A total of £1,010 million was spent on books, newspapers, magazines, cinema tickets, broadcasting licences and rentals, not including the sets themselves and the vast array of related leisure products, many of which derive from the same industrial complex.

Companies have increasingly combined to form large holdings and have diversified their interests within these large organizations. The resulting effect is that the mass media constantly reinforces itself. A vast and powerful leisure industry has grown up around the mass media. Popular or 'pop' music has proved to be a marketable and very profitable product. In brief, technology has provided the necessary hardware for promoting and sustaining this industry on a scale previously not possible.

The early promotion of music as an ideal consumer package was already evident in the late 1950s when 'pop' music proved to be a powerful commercial product with the teenage market. Palmer (1970, p. 16) goes so far as to state that:

> 'Pop' has become the most powerful selling medium of all time. 'Pop' is essentially the language of profit. Such, it might appear, is its price of acceptance.

Brief comments have already been made about the teenager's strong feeling for identity and group homogeneity. Erikson (1950, pp. 261–63) describes the 'identity crisis' which makes the adolescent so vulnerable to commercial pressure. It is apparent that this age group temporarily overidentifies with heroes of cliques and crowds: it tends to be clannish with adolescents stereotyping themselves, their ideals and their enemies. Hoffer (1974) describes various factors which have contributed to this vulnerability — that adolescents live for the present, have increasingly more leisure time and are often employed in unsatisfying occupations. Significantly they are a sizeable part of the population, have comparatively large amounts of money to spend and live in an industrial society which has constantly extended the span of adolescence.

It is generally believed pop music's importance to youth is sociological rather than aesthetic and used mainly as a means of identity with the peer group. It has also been suggested that teenage culture, being highly emotional and essentially non-verbal, is therefore more naturally expressed through the 'beat' and 'drive' of pop music, dancing and dress (Hall and Whannel 1964, p. 282). Accordingly these expressive outlets have been commercially exploited to impose and manipulate taste, as for example in 1961 when the 'twist' was first introduced as a dance. Promoted through the dance hall, press, television, film, record and publication, commercial fashion houses produced 'twist' dresses, 'twist' shoes and 'twist' necklaces.

As with other consumer goods, the majority of pop music and its performers tend to have an in-built obsolescence. Here the role of the media makes a strong contribution by helping to speed up the fashion cycle of the young. Young people tend to be specifically attentive to those media (records, tape, radio, magazines) which promote pop individuals and groups to stardom. Thus radio is a powerful influence in terms of air time which can be devoted to repetitious publicity or 'plugging'. Disc jockeys or 'link' men are promoted to star status as personalities in their own right. Magazines reinforce the pop industry by devoting coverage to the records and life stories of ascending and current pop stars. The quality of the product which these media provide appears insignificant compared with the cult of the personality and the development of what is termed 'character merchandizing'. It has been found that a human or fictional character can be promoted in such a way as to sell musical as well as other products. Character merchandizing was once associated with the nursery but it is clear that it is now a rapidly and developing world wide industry. Used to sell anything from records to lollipops, this marketing method has been found to be particularly successful with the pre-school, primary and teenage age groups. Of these, the 5 to 12-year-olds are said to be the most receptive. An example of highly successful character merchandizing with this group has been the promotion of the 'Wombles' (originally characters in a children's book) through records, toys, notepaper, soap, etc.

Pop music in all its forms has an appeal which is not only restricted to adolescents. Commercial interests have been quick to realize that younger children make excellent targets and have promoted particular pop groups to appeal to the pre-teenage group. Since the Second World War western society has experienced increased affluence and much improved living standards. Accordingly the commercial leisure industry has been able to make an impact on all age groups and the techniques of manipulating taste and fashions have proved no less successful with adults who can be similarly lured to adopt superficial views of life.

The impact of pop music is best seen with respect to specific products. For example, the post-war boom in 45 rpm singles records reached a peak in 1964 and in successive years the long playing record has steadily risen in popularity. In 1975 over 101 million long playing records were produced compared with approximately 76 million singles. Yet more recent is the phenomenal growth of recorded tape in the form of cartridges and cassettes. Eleven million of these were being produced in 1972 and now figures have more than doubled. Like the transistor radio before it, the cassette recorder has fast achieved popularity in the car and the home and is now completely transportable.

The power of electronic sound and the immediacy of its appeal first made an impact on the public with the amplified sound of the guitar in rock and roll music. Electronic music is now familiar in film track, television programmes and commercials, pop and serious works. Further development has resulted in the creation of the Moog synthesizer which enables music to be programmed and played live without recording or tape editing. As Douglas points out (1973, p. 102), the composer can now be his own performer, an omnipotent being who has no need to score music or to hire musicians. Any sound within the limits of audibility is available and he is able to modify or rewrite at will. A supreme example of today's sophisticated recording techniques is the recording of Mike Oldfield's 'Tubular Bells' in which the composer plays every instrument and achieves a total effect by effective 'overdubbing'. Electronic music studios are now commonplace in colleges, polytechnics and universities. It would appear that this type of composition demands a new kind of hybrid musician who needs to be scientifically equipped with a knowledge of electronic terminology, audio acoustics and mathematics, in addition to his conventional musical skills.

Mass production of electronic organs and keyboard units has been the resulting spin-off from this type of development. Once a feature of the cinema and more latterly in the church, the electronic organ is now common to both stage and home. Incorporated into the design are many automatic features: rhythm units, chord, automatic bass and arpeggios; and synthesis sounds such as strings, trombone and trumpet effects. Estimated to be worth approximately 15 to 20 million pounds, the electronic organ industry markets about 25 different makes of instrument. In addition there are many miniature instruments, including table models, which are available in popular chain stores. With a price ranging from around £30 (6-button) to a £50 (12-button) larger model, harmony can be obtained by selecting the appropriately lettered button and the melodic line by playing from numbered keys. Accompanying 'teach yourself' manuals enable one to become an instant performer without the rigour of learning conventional notation or acquiring physical technique. Man has become a technician making music by numbers in much the same way as he handles a pocket calculator.

Murray Schafer (1973, p. 27) believes that *the* most striking feature of twentieth-century music is the blurring of edges between music and environmental sounds. Sound in all its forms saturates the environment. Packaged or 'convenience' music is everywhere, in the supermarket, lift, restaurant and dental surgery. Used as an opiate in this way, a non-listening habit is rapidly becoming the norm. To many people music functions as an insignificant background rather like wallpaper. Schafer (1973, p. 27) contends that the increasing use of packaged sound as pioneered by the Muzak corporation has split sound from the sound maker, so that we are now in a state of 'schizophonia'. This state, he believes (Schafer 1973, p. 27), can only be improved if everyone concerned with the improvement of the environment were to work towards the recovery of positive silence.

> I am about to suggest that the soundscape will not again become ecological and harmonious until silence is recovered as a positive and felicitous state in itself. We need to regain that state in order that fewer sounds could intrude on it with pristine brilliance.

Inevitably the effect of mass culture and its artificially stimulated standards affects the work of schools. Hoffer (1974) has examined certain features of youth pop music which militate against the music teacher wishing to inculcate an appreciation of art music. These are its all pervasiveness, leading to the inevitable non-listening habit and its high volume. In comparison 'art' music is said to appear like a slow motion film of an athletic contest.

Perhaps of greater danger than bad pop music is the clearly evident acceptance of what may be termed 'convenience' music. Bland, displaying constant regularity of beat, monotonous repetition of rhythmic pattern, convenience music lacks the essential dissonance/resolution that gives impulse to artistic form. This type of music is however becoming increasingly accepted in both educational broadcast and in the classroom. Television programmes for mothers and children at home have also displayed this trend. Marshall (1972) states 'there is a tendency to provide too much ephemeral music on such programmes, resulting in a stream of musical trivialities and clichés.

Swanwick (1968) describes how in the early 60s the Beatles gave pop music a much needed injection of gaiety, zest and musical quality. In addition, it is fair to say that a wider acceptance of musical styles has brought the guitar into schools as well as brass bands, jazz bands, dance bands, steel bands and ensembles of great diversity. Within an educational context this acceptance relies heavily on a teacher's discrimination to judge what is good pop, good jazz, good folk or good modern music. And it is this which Hall and Whannel (1964, p. 37) stress — 'the task of education is essentially one of discrimination'. This is certainly the case in the 1970s when the recording industry is making an overwhelming impact by the sheer quantity of music it produces. It would appear that never before have there been such individual opportunities for participating in musical activity or listening to music of all kinds. Yet, it cannot be ignored that the mass taste which the commercial leisure industry helps to promote may well be exerting a powerful counterbalance to set against a whole range of positive initiatives.

Chapter 7
The changing face of education

> There is nothing more difficult to take in hand, more perilous to
> conduct or more uncertain in its success than to take the lead in the
> introduction of a new order of things.
>
> MACHIAVELLI, *The Prince*

In concluding this account of recent developments in music education, it
seems appropriate to group summary observations into three general
areas. First, there is a brief recapitulation of significant factors which
appear to have influenced the status of music in education. Second, there
follows a description of emerging trends and potential opportunities for
promoting music education in the school and community. Finally,
particular issues are identified where greater professional commitment
could improve the long term value of music within the educational
context.

Re-appraisal

Through the driving force of the sight-singing movement, music, one of
the oldest curriculum subjects, came to be established in the new state
system of education in the nineteenth century. So too the other tradition
of private music tuition was reinforced by the development of external
local examinations administered by the music conservatoires. The
resulting dualism on the one hand may have helped to weaken music's
status in the school context, yet on the other served to promote vigorous
musical growth in the community as a whole.

Several other factors appear to have militated against music's progress
in schools up to the last decade. By at first excluding music from
matriculation status the universities effectively devalued music's importance in the Grammar School. This restricted the supply of future music
teachers. Music's later inclusion and the need to reinforce its academic
aspects imposed a dominant theoretical framework on the subject. Again,
the teacher's frequent isolation within his institution and the varied
training background of many teachers effectively acted as a deterrent
from forming a balanced professional concensus on curriculum goals and
objectives. It is only very recently that educational studies in music have
received any serious attention for almost all the older universities have
tended to disregard the study of musical pedagogy at both undergraduate
and postgraduate level. As a result, for many years trained school music
specialists have been in short supply both in the secondary and primary
sectors. In the infant school the shortage has not been so apparent for
here educational philosophy has tended to support a non-specialist policy.

One could also argue that the early success of school music broadcasts provided a too convenient substitute for specialized teaching personnel.

Post-war affluence and the expanding resources of the late 50s and 60s wrought many changes. The appointment of music advisers, the development of instrumental teaching schemes and music centres, youth ensembles and festivals, have resulted in a burgeoning of instrumental performance at all levels. Visiting or peripatetic teachers have become part of the educational system. A consequent broadening of the music curriculum since 1965 has been boosted by the introduction of the alternative Certificate of Secondary Education (CSE), the establishment of several new university departments and the creation of polytechnic music schools. Practical performance is now an integral part of the music degree course as is provision for specialization at undergraduate level. Student numbers have increased dramatically during this period and there is now considerable choice between music degree courses and combinations with other subjects. Adult or 'recurrent' education is fast becoming a growth area, a movement owing much to the impact of the Open University and its innovative approach to distance learning.

During this period several influences have affected the music curriculum. As an academic discipline research into music psychology and music education has now begun to develop in the United Kingdom. The pioneering work of Wing and Bentley has been reinforced by initiatives from the new universities, particularly from the University of York, where musical pedagogy is a strong feature of the curriculum and research activity already well established. Further impetus has come from the growth of child developmental studies and from such international influences as the music educators Orff, Kodály and Suzuki. With society's concern for the needs of the individual the therapeutic value of music and the arts has assumed increasing importance both as a curative and remedial tool and, latterly, in its cathartic sense. A trend for 'creativity' in terms of self-expression as well as originality has been assisted by individual music teachers, art education and philosophical writings. This has gradually promoted a shift of emphasis towards the 'affective' value of music and the arts. The recognition of the catalytic effect which one art can have on another has led to more detailed exploration of their integrative possibilities within the context of the school curriculum and at advanced level.

Pressures on the school curriculum have come from diverse sources. Educational agencies and government reports have highlighted particular areas of concern. The Schools Council has sponsored two music projects on curriculum reform and innovation. Music in the community has benefited greatly from the achievements of the BBC, increased public spending and, more recently, from commercial sponsorship. A general raising of musical standards, both in provision and appreciation, may now be resulting from regionalism and the devolution movement.

Emerging trends — potential opportunities

The last few years have seen rapid change in educational organization as teaching institutions begin to adapt to the needs of a wider community. Reorganization of secondary school education into large comprehensive units is resulting in the amalgamation of many existing schools and the building of new institutions. For the music teacher this building programme brings planned purpose-built facilities such as music suites and music centres on a scale hitherto unknown. Large music rooms, smaller areas for group performance and practice rooms are now acoustically designed so that the timetabling of instrumental activity is seen to be a practical proposition.

Another benefit now emerging from this trend towards larger units is that the music teacher no longer works in isolation but is increasingly part of a team within a sizeable music department. This situation inevitably demands greater organization and curriculum planning, at the same time presenting opportunities for sharing ideas and expertise within new hierarchical structures. As part of this team the peripatetic teacher now has a vital role. To a large extent the visiting teacher has become the 'new professional' leaving behind the image of the private teacher whose status was derived from a valued place in the community and the obligatory nameplate by the door.

In larger comprehensive schools separate arts departments are often combined to form departments of 'creative' or 'expressive' arts. For example, these often incorporate the departments of art, music, dance, drama, photography and film. In this way, the specialist music teacher works as part of an extended team with its potential for strengthening the status of music alongside the other arts within the school curriculum.

Another emerging trend is that of collaboration where individual schools pool their resources in order to make advanced work more effective. Sixth form centres are being developed which enable advanced level courses in subjects such as music to be a viable and efficient use of manpower. Bristol, for example, is an area where advanced level music, resources and manpower have been in short supply. Here an advanced music school has been established (Maconie 1975a) where pupils from over twenty schools can pursue music 'A' level studies with highly specialized teaching, superior equipment and the concentration of interest which work with a musical peer group can bring to this level of study.

The need for more efficient and imaginative use of resources is leading to the use of educational establishments as resource centres for the surrounding community. Milton Keynes, for example, has planned its Stantonbury Education and Leisure Campus for this particular purpose, as the name suggests. Advertisements for music teachers are now beginning to stress the commitment which is required to community education and the opportunities which this presents for working with adults as well as children.

Tertiary institutions too, which have been traditionally concerned with the training of teachers for primary or secondary work, are now beginning to reshape their future in the light of drastically reduced student intakes and even threats of closures. They are now beginning to expand into community education by providing music resources where performance and teaching facilities are made available on payment of an annual fee. As a consequence it may be that many music centres and arts establishments which have been formerly concerned with child and youth education may also extend their facilities to the whole community.

Education and culture are no longer seen to be the exclusive preserve of school or concert hall. Efforts have been made throughout Europe in recent years to establish a policy which regards culture and cultural development as integral to human life as daily sustenance (Jor 1976). This 'democratisation' or 'demystification' of culture has led, since 1967, to a mushroom-like growth of some 149 community arts centres in the United Kingdom alone, together with several similar developments in the rest of Europe. Here, at centres such as the Cockpit, Marylebone, the Trinity Arts Centre, Birmingham, and many others, people of all ages are encouraged to become involved in devising, directing and participating in musical, dramatic and other arts events. Jor states (1976, p. 110)

> The interesting fact about the existing creative activities is that they have emerged without having been previously thought out. They have established a cultural goal without having been told that creativity is the fuel of culture.

Although it is in inner urban areas where the need for community arts provision seems greatest, rural and village communities have expressed similar needs. Interesting ventures have already taken place. For example, aided by an Arts Council grant, the village of Blewbury in Oxfordshire commissioned an opera tailor-made to its own requirements. Everyone in the village participated in some aspect of the total cultural experience — performance, administration or costume making. This country has a long and valuable tradition of amateur choirs, orchestras, operatic and dramatic societies. In a sense, the new community arts movement builds on this tradition of self-help and motivation thereby extending cultural activities to a great number of people who, otherwise, might never come into contact with such experiences.

The Arts Council and the Regional Arts Associations are currently providing financial aid for about 100 community arts projects. At the time of writing it has just been announced that the Arts Council is to give an additional £40,000 to the £1,300,000 already allocated for the year 1978–9 in order to increase the accessibility of the arts to the general public. In view of these developments the introduction of a new two year DipHE course on 'Music and the Community' at Dartington College of Arts is a timely innovation.

The discernible trend towards recognizing the importance of life-long education or *l'education permanente* and the use of leisure time clearly has implications for the musical needs of the community. Traditionally many of these needs have been met by extra-mural classes, the BBC radio and the enthusiastic self help of groups like gramophone societies, amateur operatic groups etc. Yet the emphasis is shifting to provide courses dealing with the basic elements of music, enabling people to 'do' rather than talk about music. Increasingly these requirements are being fostered by radio educational broadcasts, the Open University and other adult education establishments such as Nene College, Morley College, Goldsmiths and the City Literary Institute. With the success of the Open University as a large-scale provider of the 'second chance' there is now a greater motivation to pursue courses leading to a diploma or a degree giving the desired 'sanctity of an award' with external 'currency' value.

It has been prophesied that 'By the end of the century people would have twice the leisure and twice the amount of money to spend on it ...' (Burns 1968).

To this should be added the anticipation of increased life expectancy and the potential needs of a vast number of young people who will emerge into adulthood having enjoyed the benefits of instrumental playing in school and youth orchestras. It is therefore surprising that literature on sociological aspects of leisure neglects the place of music and the arts in society. Unlike leisural publications of the 1930s which responded to the advent of the media, latterday studies make scant reference to music's place as a leisure activity. One writer has pointed to the lack of information on audience figures for concert, opera and ballet attendance (Parker 1976, p. 126). There will evidently be an increasing need for statistical information of this nature in order to plan most effectively for music and the arts as an increasingly prominent leisure activity.

The general public now has more access to music, musical products and educational kits than at any time in history. As some of the negative features of the leisure industry have already been described its beneficial side effects and potential educational opportunities should also be identified.

Records devoted to serious or classical music are more accessible than ever before. Regardless of fashion in the world of pop music, classical records maintain a reliable ten per cent of the total record turnover and many budget-priced long playing records have appeared on the market. A wider and constantly expanding range of musical instruments is also becoming available ranging from recorders, kazoos, xylophones, guitars of all description, drum kits and electronic instruments to orchestral instruments scaled down in size and price for child and student players.

Well over one hundred music periodicals and magazines disseminate information about every aspect of music, its composers and performers. The whole spectrum of musical interest is represented ranging from pop music in all its styles in the *Melody Maker* and the 'reggae' and 'soul' of the *Black Music* magazine to the reviews and research articles on serious music and composers found in *Music and Letters* and *Music Review*. A fairly recent venture is the appearance of the first weekly classical music magazine for the general public. The coverage of *Classical Music Weekly* includes news of live and recorded music, opera and dance, interviews and criticisms together with comprehensive coverage of musical events throughout the United Kingdom. In addition, considerable information and publicity about local and regional music is available in the pamphlets, magazines and broadsheets published by the regional arts associations and leisure services departments which are freely available in local libraries. Publishing has expanded at a rapid rate and the vast quantities of books published annually are beginning to create an interesting and beneficial side effect: bargain book stores are opening up over the country where publishers' remaindered books, including music titles, can be bought at very modest prices.

Television's power to promote the cult of the personality has also proved to be effective in popularizing serious music as well as astronomy and science. André Previn successfully popularizes the classical repertoire in this way. Similarly, in his all too short life, David Munrow, a musician with charismatic personality, transmitted his enthusiasm for early music to a very wide audience. By sharing his excitement and expertise for the music of the Middle Ages and the Renaissance a broader and more knowledgeable audience has been created. This, in turn, has led to a greater demand for records, cassettes and further information on this subject.

Although the current growth of the 'Early Music' movement in schools is clearly linked with the Dolmetsch family, the present regeneration and expansion which is taking place can be very largely attributed to the influence of David Munrow. Already an Early Music Centre has opened where classes are held for children and adults and plans are underway for in-service courses, touring recitals and the publishing of resource materials. *Music in Education* recently devoted a large supplement to early music, covering the making and buying of instruments such as shawms, crumhorns and sackbuts, and extensive bibliographies of music in print and on record (*Music in Education* 1977 July/August).

Television's potential as a medium for general education has proved highly successful in the adult literacy scheme 'On the Move'. A similar programme aimed at fostering musical literacy could parallel this initiative and would obviously prove of immense benefit to music education. Music's transmission today is so intensely 'aural' that the printing of music has come to be regarded as a highly specialized process. Yet it is not so long ago that popular sheet music could be readily purchased in Woolworth stores. Ladybird, the publisher of widely read children's pocket books, has already printed music for the first time. This innovation presents a simple opportunity for children and parents to become familiar with the notation of music in almost a subliminal way and at nominal cost.

The media have the capacity to revive and regenerate interest in styles and art forms. Interest in traditional material and folk song is often regenerated in this way. Publications and records serve to feed traditional songs back into the folk movement in such as way as to both preserve and strengthen almost forgotten legacies (Myer 1974). The accelerated pace of travel and greater mobility of the population is already leading to an increased awareness and interest in the folk song and traditions of other peoples. This is shown in *Ears and Eyes*, the successor to the Oxford School Music Books series, the interest in the sitar fostered by Yehudi Menuhin and the Beatles, and in the content of many anthropological programmes on television and radio.

In the classroom teachers are already beginning to capitalize on their pupils' interest in and knowledge of the media. One aspect of this is seen in the development of pop music in the secondary school curriculum. It is now an examinable CSE subject and an optional course in several universities and colleges. Reviews of pop records and of publications about pop music are also included in the columns of the professional journals *Music in Education* and *Music Teacher*. The history of pop music from its origins in Afro-American folk song is receiving detailed study and has been treated at length by Burnett (1972). Indeed, the varied range of idioms which pop music embraces is beginning to be appreciated as a vital repertoire of authentic and often fundamental forms of musical expression. In fact, much of the more successful and worthwhile material appears to stem either from traditional song form or is based on elemental ostinato patterns. The term 'pop' is used to describe a vast area of music. As clear distinctions between pop and serious music become more difficult to make, as modern music becomes more and more ephemeral in terms of artistic 'happenings' and the incorporation of chance elements, such justifications may no longer be necessary. Eventually all music may be recognized in its own qualitative right and not justified in the curriculum solely on the strength of age and established position.

Books, encyclopaedias, quiz books on pop music and its celebrities are readily available on the general market. However, the educational use of pop music is still so innovative that, as yet, there are perhaps only three books aimed at the teaching profession. The first is a theoretical and practical guide (Swanwick 1968), the second a series of essays (Vulliamy and Lee 1976) and the third a workbook designed for use with third to sixth year secondary pupils (Attwood and Farmer 1977). Attwood (1977) has provided a comprehensive bibliography on publications and resources. The contents demonstrate that secondary school pupils now have the opportunity to draw on a wide range of pop music and its related materials. An opportunity such as this for capitalizing on pupils' interests and motivation should, at least, receive considered thought and attention.

Music teachers already pioneering this approach in the classroom report that pop music can act as a starting point, or trigger, for many different musical activities (Farmer 1976). Their experience has shown that it can often lead to exploring other areas of knowledge and that their pupils do learn how to be 'discriminative' as well as 'self-expressive'.

Music teachers can now draw upon a vast but expensive range of educational technology. The record players, tape recorders which only twelve years ago were regarded as classroom novelties are now being supplemented by an extensive array of sophisticated communication aids. Most notable is the introduction of the Piano Laboratory which, for aural work and general musicianship holds out interesting possibilities. Here, several individuals equipped with headphones can work at separate consoles without disturbing neighbouring classrooms. At a master console the teacher can give individual instruction to as many as twelve students at a time. Another aid, the audio-visual stave, has shown exceptional potential as a tool for sight-singing, work in pitch and harmony, and for keyboard harmony when coupled to the console units (Swanwick 1972). This electronic development appears to offer more prospects for pro-gramming individualized instruction, particularly in encouraging basic music concepts and literacy skills.

Another opportunity for individualized learning is presented by the 'audio book'; its use has already been applied to musical appreciation. By means of a cassette, book material can be provided in more accessible form, carefully structured and presented to avoid irritation and boredom as the content is intended to be heard over and over again.

The strong cultural effect of the media and an increasingly sophisti-cated technology inevitably will demand from teachers greater knowledge and expertise in their use and application. To use them effectively Aicken (1975) has emphasized the teacher's role as a director, script writer and actor. In-service courses in communication studies are, as yet, few and far between although they appear to have particular relevance for teachers. In view of the impact on society wrought by the media and technological change, more attention could be focused on the advantages which they offer to education and use these to further educational objectives.

Current issues

Much remains to be done to foster the long term progress of music in education. In terms of manpower and material resources considerable imbalance exists between the primary and secondary school sector. This state of affairs is further compounded by similar variations between the local authorities and the schools themselves. For every school that appears to be well equipped with advisory music staff and a wide range of musical instruments there may be several with neither musically qualified staff nor practical resources. Alongside the increasingly popular Orff instruments the much used and abused recorder still holds a firm place in school music making and has even been viewed as the 'greatest instrumental movement in the whole history of music' (Bergmann 1969, p. 15).

The organization and content of the music curriculum could benefit enormously from a regular interchange of music specialists between the primary and secondary sectors. Indeed it could be made mandatory for intending secondary school specialists to spend the early years of their teaching careers in primary schools. General concern is shown about the lack of continuity between primary and secondary school music. If, as it has been suggested, each child were to have a record card showing his personal musical achievement, the problem of school transfer might be considerably lessened (Bentley 1975, p. 24).

A considerable amount of concentrated effort has been applied to the needs of the secondary school. It may be that much of this effort is spent in fighting a rear-guard action. What are the real needs of adolescents? Are they more deserving of attention than the needs of less prominent age groups? To what extent is the adolescent phase an inevitable problem stage or is much of the music curriculum development for this group in reality a compensatory measure for earlier musical deprivation? As a nation we appear to pay lip-service to the ideals of laying good foundations while consistently preserving a system whereby music specialists are employed at secondary and tertiary levels but very rarely in the primary school. One could say that teachers of young children should be as musically able, if not more so, than those who teach older children and students. Lawrence (1975, p. 3) voices the opinion of many music educators in stating that the interests of music education are best served by concentrating on the total structure. It may well be that no substantial improvements will be made until a pyramid structure is an organizational reality, with good specialized music teaching at the basic nursery–primary level leading to music centres, specialized music schools and finally to sophisticated systems of advanced music education. The educational systems of countries such as Hungary, the USSR and Czechoslovakia appear to be based on just such a structure which makes 'music for everyone' (Kodály) a common goal while, at the same time, enabling individuals to pursue their own separate paths to excellence.

The preceding paragraphs have been mainly concerned with organizational and structural problems. Within the music profession itself there has been for too long a basic lack of unity. A major hindrance to producing clear-cut, realistic objectives is the difficulty of unifying so many diversely trained music specialists. One hopeful step in the right direction has been the formation, quite recently, of the United Kingdom Council for Music Education, the first comprehensive national body to represent the profession internationally and to act as a co-ordinating agency for the various organizations concerned with music education in this country.

Again there have been few initiatives taken in the universities to recognize the importance of pedagogic studies in the curriculum and, as a result, research into music in education is still in its infancy. In this regard, the appointment in 1976 of the first Professor of Music Education at the Institute of Education (University of London) is a significant landmark and sign of healthy growth. There have been only two major curriculum development projects on music in education, both based in universities. These have tended to be polarized in terms of their philosophical standpoint, a situation which might so easily have been improved if there were several other curriculum development projects underway and perhaps if they were attached to various types of institutions. Clearly general interest in musical pedagogy is not enough and research activity is impeded by a lack of research workers and appropriate funding. For example, this is an area where commercial firms (already sponsoring musical events) might be persuaded to fund modestly priced projects on specific aspects of music curriculum development.

Our educational system gives teachers an unlimited amount of freedom in the way they teach their subject. And indeed the imposition of any particular teaching method and philosophy is not practised in the British educational system. Paradoxically this very freedom can be a strait-jacket for the newly qualified teacher is armed with a set of general principles which he is expected to effectively relate and apply to any given situation. Here one might agree with the view of Simpson (1969) who states that many of us only come to understand general principles through contact with a considerable number of particular instances. Music education clearly needs more methods and guidelines, not less, wherever relevant applying and adapting the practices of successful educators. Teaching methods are now receiving attention which are based on the use of colour or number such as the Tobin Colour Music System (Cooper 1976), the Hubicki (1972) 'Colour Staff' and the Justine Ward Method (More 1968). The Tower Hamlets Music Centre in London is using a method of string teaching devised by Dr Paul Rolland of the University of Illinois which emphasizes musical games and group activities. All these methods need to be examined, re-examined and evaluated so that any new teacher is equipped to make realistic comparisons and practical choice. It is too expensive to expect teachers to devise their own methods or constantly struggle in what may be fruitless experimentation. Yet by building on proven practice, on the 'known' a personal approach is usually more successfully and more confidently evolved.

A comparative neglect of singing as a classroom activity has become apparent as more and more instrumentally biased teachers have entered the schools. Bentley (1975) emphasizes the importance of using the voice as a first instrument to cultivate what he describes as 'tonal' thinking, where a sound is pitched in the head before being produced vocally or on an instrument. The opposite process, 'peripheral' musical thinking, occurs when an instrument is manipulated to produce a sound which is then perceived by the brain. Recent developments in electronic sound sources are even further removed from the human body. There is mounting concern about the danger of neglecting vocal skills, sight reading and aural training at all levels. Clements (1974) points to the successful achievements of the nineteenth-century tonic sol-fa movement and emphasizes the point that the systematic teaching of sight-singing is just as relevant in today's infant schools. There is considerable support for the value of sol-fa training as a systematic approach to aural work at all levels of music education which would give many students better opportunities for realizing their full potential. The revival of the Curwen Institute, with its new examination structure is an initiative taken to reassert the value of tonic sol-fa as a vital element in music education. If increased attention can be directed to these efforts and to the potential application of equally rigorous training systems, such as the Kodály Method, there is every reason to foresee a significant raising of educational standards.

The long term interests of music in education have so often been sacrificed to fashion and expediency. Recently the search for 'creativity' in musical activity (in the sense of both 'originality' and 'exploration') appears to have received a disproportionate amount of the timetable. At the risk of over simplificiation, the paramount need in music education, as in education generally, is for a sense of balance in the curriculum. This is not necessarily a plea for more music in the school timetable but for better utilization of the music lesson in terms of skilful and imaginative teaching which encompasses a greater range of musical activities.

There is the need to teach children about a musical tradition and the skills it demands, at the same time providing the means whereby they can develop, adapt or possibly discard that tradition as they grow in confidence and individuality. It is imperative that musical foundations be sound and laid in the early years to obviate much compensatory and remedial work in later life. There should be, and always will be, differing approaches, a spectrum of rationales and, one would hope, a professional commitment to constant values and balance in the face of changing trends and fashions.

But there are clearly major issues, other than those concerned with curriculum content. Up until now an almost exclusive emphasis has been placed on the educational requirements of the primary and secondary schools and the conventional routes to higher education. A drastically falling birthrate combined with increased life expectancy is causing educational planners to formulate new policies and new philosophies for this changing population pattern. At the 1978 Annual Conference of the Convention of Scottish Local Authorities Professor John Stewart forecast that, in the coming years the population would at best remain static for ten years; the number of school children would go down by some 25 per cent while the aged population would rise by about 20 per cent.

One would not need to be a fortune teller to predict that within the next ten years there will be a major shift of emphasis from the school system and its requirements to those of the whole life cycle. This more comprehensive view of society's educational needs is already drawing the attention of music educators and arts administrators to hitherto neglected sections of the population: the pre-school area, highly gifted children, the 16 to 19-year-olds (outside the school system), ethnic minority groups and adults of all ages.

The pre-school area

Earlier, reference was made to the lack of specialized music education at the pre-school level. Certain innovative developments are taking place however. Moog's (1976) seminal work on the musical experience of the pre-school child is now available in an English translation. Musicians are beginning to experiment with instrumental teaching for the young child, along the lines of the Suzuki Method. The Open University, in one of its Associate Courses, has produced structured material for adults to use with pre-school children, including instruction on early music learning and a record suggesting appropriate musical activities. As so often happens one subject area can be reinforced by another and so music education is being aided by the work of psychologists and the medical profession. Dr Audrey Wisbey (1977) has developed a programme of musical and auditory training designed to assist children in acquiring basic literacy skills. By isolating musical concepts such as pitch, duration, intensity and tone quality, the elements of speech sound are learnt in a simple and structured manner. Medical research is also underway into the pitch and rhythm of sounds experienced by babies in the womb and the effect of music after birth. These endeavours will inevitably add momentum to promoting music education in the pre-school sector.

Highly gifted children

This account has dealt substantially with aspects of music provision for the majority of children. It has also identified the special needs of the handicapped and the slow learners, at the risk of neglecting the small, yet significant, proportion of highly gifted children. These, too, need identification, encouragement and special provision so as to counteract the likelihood that they might be deprived of equal opportunities for development. The specialist music schools, already described, are few in number. First rate teachers tend to be concentrated in the big cities and financial support from LEAs fluctuates considerably from area to area.

The problem particularly stressed by the recent Gulbenkian Report (1978) and the government discussion paper on gifted children (Department of Education and Science 1977) is that of adequately identifying potentially gifted musicians at an early age. Again, this problem could be alleviated by establishing a policy of specialist music teaching and advice in the pre-school and primary sectors.

The 16 to 19-year-olds outside the school system

This is another section of the population whose educational requirements are seen to be in urgent need of attention. Many of the children leaving school at sixteen have been involved in orchestras, bands and ensembles. All too often they suddenly become isolated from educational opportunities and musical activities in particular. This is a European problem as well as a British one and the Organization for Economic and Cultural Development (OECD 1977) forecasts a general policy trend which will offer the school leaver far greater access to educational opportunities than he has at present.

Ethnic minority groups

Naseem Khan's report *The Arts Britain Ignores* (Khan 1976) revealed the extensive but unrecognized wealth of ethnic minority culture in Britain. It is clear that the music of ethnic minority groups could and should figure more prominently than it does in the main stream of British musical life. In the light of the government's announcement that it will draw up guidelines for a new curriculum fitting the needs of a multi-racial society, the collection, dissemination and adaptation of ethnic music would be of immense benefit to music education. In a wider sense UNESCO (1977, pp. 304–5) has stressed the importance of preserving one's cultural heritage as a major contribution towards affirming cultural uniqueness and self-respect.

> One can not, therefore, overemphasize the fact that the idea of cultural heritage in the broadest sense, not only the visible and material manifestations of this heritage ... but also the oral traditions, *the musical and ethnographic heritage* ... expresses the essence of ethnic or national temperament.

Here, music's potential as an integrative and harmonizing force should not be undervalued in this movement towards recognizing the needs and aspirations of minority groups.

Adult education

Many interesting developments which have been taking place in adult or 'lifelong' education in music have already been described. Adult education generally has been brought into focus by the Russell Report (Department of Education and Science 1973) and the innovations of the Open University. It has been said by Redcliffe-Maud (1976, p. 23) that

> ... within the next five years or so, the adult education movement must receive priority such as it has had at no time in our history.

Increasing provision will need to be made to meet a continuing and expanding demand both for vocational courses and the non-vocational courses by which adults are often drawn into the educational system.

Within the next ten years the adult education movement could be greatly assisted by the effects of the declining birthrate which will have worked through to the institutions of higher education. The government has just produced a discussion paper (Department of Education and Science 1978) which deals with the implications to higher education of falling enrolment in the 1980s (see Table 4). From necessity tertiary institutions will need to set their sights on a broader and more innovatory recruitment policy. Several suggestions, therefore, contained in models *d* and *e* of this document, if implemented, would certainly open the door to wider adult education opportunities.

One suggestion offered is that there should be encouragement to provide and take up two rather than three-year courses (DipHE) and that accelerated degree courses might be offered. Another alternative is to divert attention from full-time to part-time education assisted by longer periods of paid educational leave. It is foreseen that there might be greater participation in higher education by children of manual workers, assisted by a new climate of educational opportunity and from comprehensive school reorganization. It accepts that the demand for a system of continuing education is already being felt and that there should be more systematic access to recurrent education assisted by forms of paid leave or more generous in-service grants.

The neglect of in-service education has been a bone of contention for many years. According to present estimates (OECD 1977) only between 2,000 and 3,000 teachers a year attend courses of one term or one year out of a total teaching force of over 400,000, a proportion of less than one per cent. Back in 1972 teachers were being offered the prospect of a period of one term's leave for every seven years of service (Department of Education and Science 1972a). For economic reasons this plan has never been implemented. However, the Department of Education and Science has recently begun a special survey on 'Paid Educational Leave' (PEL) and one might hope that suitable provision for in-service training and recurrent education will soon be made. Much could be learnt from American example. For many years in the USA teachers have been

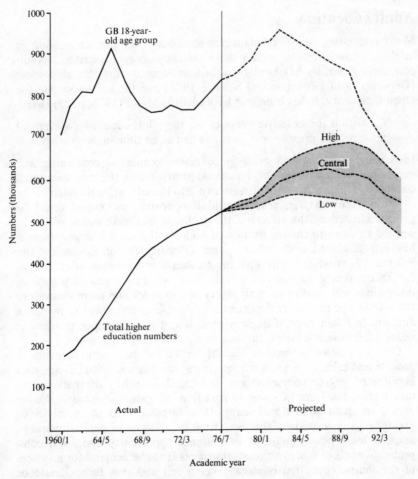

TABLE 4 18-year-old population and total full-time and sandwich students in higher education in Great Britain.

Source Higher Education into the 1990s. DES London 1978

encouraged to pursue higher qualifications lured by the prospect of higher retirement pensions. This monetary incentive ensures that those who might otherwise receive a permanent teaching licence for life do not become out of date or complacent through lack of systematic recurring educational opportunities.

The way ahead

Since 1965 great strides have been made in broadening, enhancing and diversifying the music curriculum within the educational system. Research studies and curriculum development have begun to have some impact on music education. Clearly if this momentum can be carried forward there is every reason to be optimistic of music's improved educational role and status in coming years.

Music education will be concerned much more with the individual's needs throughout the complete life cycle rather than with narrowly defined phases such as childhood, adolescence, youth and early adulthood. Certainly new avenues to learning will combine with more traditional patterns to form richer and more varied educational alternatives. As we have seen, music education has never been the sole preserve of the school system and this fact should enable the music teaching profession to adjust, perhaps better than many other subject specialists, to the changing pattern of educational development. Where past policies have endeavoured to make music education accessible to all children of school age, future policy may enable everyone, regardless of age, to have ever expanding opportunities and greater access to music throughout life.

Appendix I
Landmarks in music education

General events	Landmarks in music
1870 Elementary Education Act passed. Board schools established.	Sight-singing mania sweeps the country.
1872	Curwen's 'New Standard Course' published. Hullah made first government inspector for music.
1873	Curwen's Tonic Sol-fa College founded. Music department established at Manchester University.
1874	Royal Musical Association founded. Music department established at University College, Aberystwyth.
1876	Holiday music courses begin at Tonic Sol-fa College. At same institution McNaught begins string classes using Curwen's String Band Book.
1879	External examination system inaugurated by Trinity College. National Union of Musical Instrument Makers founded.
1880 Mundella Act ensures compulsory attendance at school until 10 years of age.	
1881	Royal Academy of Music introduces its own external examination system.
1882	Society of Professional Musicians founded (later becomes the Incorporated Society of Musicians).
1883	Music department established at Cardiff (University College of Wales).
1885	Birmingham School of Music founded.
1887 Flat disc recording invented by Emile Berliner.	
1888	Beethoven Society founded.

General events	Landmarks in music
1889	The Royal Academy of Music and the Royal College of Music institute the Associated Board of the Royal Schools of Music for conducting local external examinations.
1892	'School Music Review' founded. Piano Manufacturers' Association formed.
1894	Miss Annie Muirhead's Concerts for Children (Hampstead and Kensington) begin.
1895	First Promenade Concert undertaken by Sir Henry Wood.
1896 First moving picture show presented in London.	
1897	Music departments established at universities of Reading and Durham.
1899	Gramophone introduced to public.
1902	Music Masters' Association founded.
1904	Association of Competitive Festivals formed.
1905	Music department established at London University (Goldsmiths).
1907	*Music Teacher* first published.
1908	Music Teachers' Association founded by Stewart Macpherson. Edward Elgar becomes first professor of music at Birmingham University.
1911	Gwynne Kimpton concerts for children begin at Aeolian Hall. Society of Women Musicians founded.
1912	First Dalcroze Eurhythmics demonstration in London.
1913	London School of Dalcroze Eurhythmics established.
1915	Music Publishers' Association formed.
1917 School Certificate Examination's first year.	
1918	Association of Musical Instrument Industries formed.

General events	Landmarks in music
1919 Sound broadcasting begins.	HMV company establish an education department. Carl Seashore's *Measures of Musical Talent* published.
1921	British Federation of Music Festivals formed. Musicians' Union formed from an amalgamation of two organizations in existence before 1900.
1922 British Broadcasting Company formed.	
1923	National Gramophonic Society founded. First year of Robert Mayer concerts for children.
1924 Schools Broadcasting begins.	Walford Davies broadcasts first radio music lessons.
1925 Electrical recording invented.	Descant recorder introduced into schools. First bamboo pipes made in schools. (Finlay Street School, Fulham). Dartington estate bought by the Elmhirsts.
1926 Report on 'The Education of the Adolescent' (Sir Henry Hadow).	Ernest Read's London Junior Orchestra formed. *Melody Maker* newspaper founded (first weekly paper on popular music). Dalcroze Society founded. Royal College of Music Saturday morning children's classes begin.
1927 The introduction of 'talking' films.	Royal School of Church Music founded. Ulric Brunner's non-competitive festival movement established. University of Sheffield establishes music department under Professor Percy Buck. BBC takes over the organization and funding of the Promenade Concerts.
1928	Music department established at Glasgow University under Dr. Whittaker.
1929	Hertfordshire Rural Music Schools' Association founded by Mary Ibberson. Pipers' Guild established by Margaret James. First county music committees formed. First music lecturer appointed at Leeds University.

General events	Landmarks in music
1931 Hadow Report on Primary Schools.	London Senior Orchestra formed by Ernest Read.
1933 Hadow Report (Infant and Nursery Schools) appeared.	
1934	Ann Driver broadcasts first 'Music and Movement' series.
1935	Founding of National Federation of Music Societies.
1936 Television broadcasting begins.	Workers' Music Association established.
1937	*Music in Schools* first published (later renamed *Music in Education*).
1938 Report on Secondary Education (Sir William Spens) published.	Schools' Music Association founded.
1939	Founding of Percussion Band Association.
1942	CEMA (Council for the Encouragement of Music and the Arts) founded.
1943 Report on Curriculum and Examinations in Secondary Schools (Sir Cyril Norwood) published.	SPNM (Society for Promotion of New Music) founded.
1944 Education Act (Butler) passed. Board of Education becomes Ministry of Education.	Music department established at the University of Newcastle.
1945	Suzuki begins his Talent Education movement in Japan. Kodály starts to build up Music Primary Schools in Hungary. CEMA becomes the Arts Council. National Youth Orchestra of Wales is founded. Composers' Society established. Ernest Read's Orchestral Concerts for Children begin.
1946	Bantock Society founded. Standing Conference for Amateur Music is formed.

General events	Landmarks in music
1946—*contd.*	Founding of Galpin Society for original research into history, construction and use of musical instruments. First music departments established at University College, Bangor and University of Bristol.
1947 School leaving age raised to fifteen.	National Youth Orchestra founded. Dartington Summer School of Music instituted. International Folk Music Council founded. Music Advisers' National Association formed. Ivor Keys appointed first professor of music at Queen's University, Belfast. Gerald Abraham appointed first professor of music at University of Liverpool. Music department established at the University of Nottingham under direction of Frank Metheringham Laming.
1948 Long playing record becomes commercially available.	Herbert D. Wing's *Test of Musical Aptitude* published. Music department established at Huddersfield Technical College.
1949	Studio 49 manufactures 'Orff' instruments in Germany. Musical Education of the Under-Twelves Association founded.
1950 Sound tape invented.	Elgar Society founded.
1951	Rose-Morris Company introduce the chime bar to Britain. Music department established at the University of Hull under the direction of R. B. Marchant.
1952	The founding of the National Schools' Brass Band Association. National Youth Brass Band is founded. A music department is established at the University of Southampton (first chair held from c. 1929–33 by Professor George Leake which then lapsed). Wagner Society founded.
1953	National Music Council of Great Britain founded. First International Music Conference takes place in Brussels.
1954	Robert Mayer's 'Youth and Music' concerts begin. Scottish Amateur Music Association founded.

General events

Landmarks in music

1955 Stereophonic tape invented.

Association of String Class Teachers formed.

Bax Society founded.

1956

British Youth Symphony Orchestra (Schools' Music Association) founded.
Calouste Gulbenkian Foundation established.

1957 School television programmes begin.
Ministry of Education Circular 323 'Liberal Education in Technical Colleges' published.

Music department established at the University of Leicester.

1958 Stereo records appear.
The 'bulge' transfers into secondary school.

Founding of British Society for Music Therapy.

Film of Suzuki children shown to the western world.
Orff-Schulwerk is introduced into British schools.

1959 Crowther Report on 15 to 18 year olds published.
Recommendation to increase supply of teachers.

Piano Publicity Association founded.

Peter Maxwell Davies becomes music master at Cirencester Grammar School.

Music department established at the Institute of Education, University of London, under direction of Kenneth Simpson.

1960 Certificate of Education course lengthened to 3 years.

Amateur Chamber Music Players' Society formed.

Music department established at North East Essex Technical College.
London College of Music Junior School opens.
Ernest Read Music Association founded.

1961

West Riding of Yorkshire appoints peripatetic guitar teachers.
Institute of Musical Instrument Technology founded.
National Association of Youth Orchestras formed.

1962

Central Tutorial School founded (later to become the Purcell School).
Association of Piano Group Teachers founded.
Delius Society formed.

General events

1963 Video tape invented.
Newsom Report (Half Our Future) recommends that school leaving age be raised to 16.

Robbins's Report on Higher Education recommends four year course leading to BEd degree.

1964 Schools Council formed.
New Bachelor of Education degree introduced.

1965 Certificate of Secondary Education examinations begin.

1966

Landmarks in music

London Opera Centre for young professional singers established.
Yehudi Menuhin School opens.

Boosey & Hawkes publish first six books on the Kodály Choral Method.
Television music lessons for primary schools begin.

Recorder and Music Magazine published.
Orff Institute opens in Salzburg, Austria.
Peter Warlock Society founded.

King's College (University of London) appoints first professor of music – Thurston Dart.
Music department established at Keele University.

'Sing for Pleasure' movement formed (a branch of the 'A Coeur Joie' choral movement.
Kite mark standard for musical instruments introduced.
'Beatlemania' phenomenon.

Music department established at the University of York under Professor Wilfred Mellers.

National Association of Youth Orchestras founded.
National Youth Jazz Orchestra established.
Department of music established at the University of East Anglia.
Leicestershire Schools Festival founded.
Association of Wind Teachers founded.
Royal Schools of Church Music establishes a chorister training scheme.
Gulbenkian Report *Making Musicians* published.
City of Leeds College of Music founded.

Academy of the BBC (Training Orchestra) established.
Suzuki's work introduced to the USA.
20 per cent increase in piano sales to schools in the United Kingdom reported.
Guitar becomes an examination subject for the Associated Board of the Royal Schools of Music.

General events

Landmarks in music

1966—*contd.*

First music teaching department established at the University of Exeter.

1967 Plowden Report (Children and their Primary Schools published).

First specialist course in Music Therapy established at the Guildhall School of Music.

Northern Universities' Joint Matriculation Board introduce a more practically weighted alternative to the 'A' level syllabus.
Furtwängler Society formed.

1968

Music and the Slow Learner Research Project initiated at Dartington (directed by David Ward and sponsored by the Standing Conference for Amateur Music).
First international seminar on Experimental Research in Music in Education at the University of Reading.

1969

Spohr Society founded.
Chethams School established as a national music school.
Liverpool University's music department is the base for first postgraduate studentship in orchestral conducting.
Music department established at the University of Sussex.
British Society for Electronic Music founded.

1970

Birmingham School of Music becomes first music conservatory to be incorporated into polytechnic.
Music department established at Surrey University.
'Pro Corda', a national association of young string players interested in chamber music, is founded.
Suzuki trained children tour England.
National Festival of Music for Youth established.
Schools Council research project begun on Music Education on Young Children at Reading University.
Wells Cathedral School starts specialist scheme for gifted violinists.
Liszt Society formed.

1971

Suzuki concerts and workshops held in London and provinces.
Music department established at the University of Lancaster.
Bruno Walter Society founded.
First 'Music for Slow Learners' course given at Dartington.

General events	Landmarks in music
1971—*contd.*	Chopin Society founded. Pimlico Comprehensive School initiates scheme for accommodating 15 children per year with special musical ability. First National Festival of Music for Youth takes place. First Dolmetsch Summer School for Recorder Teachers and Soloists held.
1972 James Report on Teacher Education and Training recommends 2 year Diploma in Higher Education and more attention to in-service education.	Rural Music Schools' Association initiates 5 year research project into Suzuki Talent Education Method of teaching violin and adapting it to the United Kingdom.
School leaving age raised to 16.	St. Mary's Junior School, Edinburgh becomes specialist music school. National Music Council inaugurates an award system to encourage the musical activities of local authorities. Northern School of Music and Royal Manchester College of Music merge to form Royal Northern College of Music.
1973	Schools Council Research Project begun in York on Music in the Secondary School Curriculum (5 year project). Full-time Dalcroze professional course begins at Morley College. Piano entries to Associated Board examinations drop. BBC take over promotion of Robert Mayer concerts.
1975 Birth rate of 602,000 recorded, the lowest since 1941.	First Primary Schools Brass Band Festival. Group of parents form Kingston Association for Music Education. United Kingdom Council for Music Education formed to represent all music associations at international gatherings. Leverhulme Trust award £9,000 grant to Keele University to help finance research fellowship for the study of electronic music. Curwen Institute Local Examinations and Diploma reinstituted. London Sinfonietta becomes first orchestra in 'residence' at Kingston Polytechnic.

General events	Landmarks in music
1975—*contd.*	Snape Maltings Training Orchestra founded.
	Early Music Centre established.
1976	Lloyds Bank sponsors National Youth Orchestra with grant of £45,000 over 3 years.
	Professor Keith Swanwick appointed as first professor of music education at the Institute of Education, University of London.
	International Festival of Youth Orchestras Foundation of Great Britain instituted.
	Willis, Faber and Dumas, international insurance brokers give University of East Anglia's Music Centre a computer for its electronic music studio.
	Scottish Opera receives £45,000 from Standard Life Assurance.
	First weekly classical music magazine published – *Classical Music*.
	Ladybird Books print music for first time.
	Groves Dictionary 5th Edition available as ten volume paperback books for first time.
	Association for Teachers of Singing formed.
	Association of Professional Music Therapists in Great Britain established.
	Hinrichsen Foundation Charity founded to facilitate performance and recording of new music and publication of research.
	BBC 'Nationwide' television programme inaugurates annual carol composition competition.
1977	Association of Professional Music Therapists formed.
	European Community Youth Orchestra founded.
	Academy of the BBC disbanded.
	Guildhall School of Music moves to new buildings in the Barbican.
	First music studentship awarded from firm for private tuition, music or instrument purchase.
	Scottish Opera-go-round financed for a year by Manpower Services Commission (to tour firms, factories etc.).
1978 The Oakes Report published on the Management of Higher Education in the Maintained Sector.	London Symphony Orchestra's performance of space music theme from film *Star Wars* wins 'Grammy' award from American Recording Industry.
	First competition takes place for the BBC Young Musician of the Year.

General events

1978—*contd.*
The Warnock Report
published on the
Education of
Handicapped Children
and Young People.

Landmarks in music

EPTA – European Piano Teachers' Association
founded.

First examinations conducted by the new London
Percussion Examinations Board.
Portsmouth City Council (aided by IBM (UK)
and Schroder Life Group) sponsor triennial String
Quartet Competition.
Gulbenkian Report *Training Musicians* published.

Appendix II
Key resources

1 Directories and handbooks

2 Selected magazines and journals

3 National agencies

4 Selected course centres

5 Selected instrument makers and/or distributors

6 Selected music publishers

7 Local contacts

1 Directories and handbooks

Music education

Music Education Handbook A Directory of Music Education in Britain with reference articles and tables. A. Jacobs (ed) London and New York, Bowker.
Music Education Review Vol. 1 M. Burnett (ed) London, Chappel & Co.

General

British Federation of Music Festivals Year Book obtainable from 106 Gloucester Place, London W1.
British Music Yearbook: a survey and directory with statistics and reference articles A. Jacobs (ed) London and New York, Bowker.
Hinrichsen's Musical Year Book obtainable from Bach House, 10–12 Baches Street, London N1.
International Music Guide D. Elley (ed) London, The Tantivy Press.
Kemps Music and Recording Industry Yearbook London, Kemps Group.
Penguin Stereo Record Guide E. Greenfield, B. Layton, I. March (eds) London, Penguin.

2 Selected magazines and journals

Black Music (monthly) IPC Specialist & Professional Press Ltd, 24–34 Meymott Street, London SE1 9LU.
Church Music (quarterly) Addington Palace, Croydon CR9 5AD.
Classical Music Weekly, 52a Floral Street, London WC2.
Early Music (quarterly) 44 Conduit Street, London W1R 0DE.
Folk Review (monthly) Austin House, Hospital Street, Nantwich, Cheshire.
Gilbert and Sullivan Journal (tri-annual) 54 Camborne Road, Morden, Surrey.
Jazz Times (monthly) 10 Southfield Gardens, Twickenham, Middlesex TW1 4SZ.
Melody Maker (weekly) IPC 24–34 Meymott Street, London SE1 9LU.
Music and Letters (quarterly) Oxford University Press, Press Road, Neasden, London NW10 0DD.
Music and Musicians (monthly) Hansom Books, PO Box 294, 2 & 4 Old Pye St, Victoria Street, London SW1.
Music Here (monthly) 7 Victoria Avenue, Sutton, Surrey KT6 5DL.
Music in Education (monthly) Macmillan Journals Ltd, 4 Little Essex Street, London WC2R 3LF.
Music Review (quarterly) Heffers Printers Ltd, King Hedges Road, Cambridge.
Music Stand (tri-annual) J. & W. Chester Ltd, Eagle Court, London EC 1M 5QD (magazine for 11–15 year olds).
Music Teacher (monthly) Evans Brothers, Montague House, Russell Square, London WC1.
Musical Quarterly G. Schirmer Inc., 866 Third Avenue, New York 10022.

Musical Times (monthly) Novello & Co. Ltd, 1–3 Upper James Street, London W1R 4BP.

New Musical Express (weekly) 128 Long Acre, London WC2E 9QH.

Recorder and Music Magazine (quarterly) 48 Great Marlborough Street, London W1.

Strad (The) (monthly) Novello & Co., 1–3 Upper James Street, London W1R 4BP.

3   National agencies

Arts Council of Great Britain   105 Piccadilly, London W1V 0AU.

Associated Board of the Royal Schools of Music   14 Bedford Square, London WC1B 3JG.

British Council (music department)   10 Spring Gardens, London SW1A 2BN.

British Federation of Music Festivals (incorporating Music Teachers' Association)   106 Gloucester Place, London W1H 3DB.

British Society for Music Therapy   48 Lanchester Road, London N6.

Calouste Gulbenkian Foundation   98 Portland Place, London W1N 4ET.

Choir Schools Association   Cathedral Choir School, Whitcliffe Lane, Ripon, Yorks HG4 2LA.

Composers Guild of Great Britain   10 Stratford Place, London W1N 9AE.

Council for Music in Hospitals   72 Shortheath Road, Farnham, Surrey.

Dalcroze Society   89 Highfield Avenue, London NW11 2RB.

Dolmetsch Foundation   14 Chestnut Way, Godalming, Surrey GU7 1TS.

English Folk Dance and Song Society   Cecil Sharp House, 2 Regent's Park Rd, London NW1 7AY.

Ernest Read Music Association   143 King Henry's Rd, London NW3 3RD.

European Piano Teachers' Association (EPTA)   28 Emperor's Gate, London SW7 4H5.

European String Teachers' Association   5 Neville Avenue, New Malden, Surrey KT3 46N.

Galpin Society   Rose Cottage, Bois Lane, Chesham Bois, Amersham, Bucks HP6 6BP.

Gilbert and Sullivan Society   273 Northfield Avenue, London W5 4UA.

Incorporated Society of Musicians   10 Stratford Place, London W1N 9AE.

International Society for Music Education (British Branch)   c/o R. Smith, Senior Music Adviser, Education Dept, Avon House North, St James Barton, Bristol BS99 7EB.

Jazz Centre Society Ltd   12 Carlton House Terrace, London SW1.

Laban Art of Movement Guild   Goldsmiths' College, London SE14.

Live Music Now   38 Wigmore Street, London W1H 9DF.

Music Advisers' National Association   c/o Peter Isherwood, Coventry School of Music, Percy St, Coventry CV1 3BY.

Music Education of the Up to Thirteens   55 Farm Close, Seaford, Sussex BN25 3RY.

Music Masters' Association   Orchard House, Benefield Rd, Oundle, Peterborough PE8 4EU.

Music Teachers' Association   106 Gloucester Place, London W1.

Musicians' Union   29 Catherine Place, London SW1E 6EH.

National Association of Youth Orchestras   30 Park Drive, Grimsby, S. Humberside DN32 0EG.

National Federation of Music Societies   1 Montague Street, London WC1B 5BF.

National Institute of Adult Education   19B De Montfort St, Leicester.

National Music Council of Gt Britain   35 Morpeth Mansions, Morpeth Terrace, London SW1P 1EU.

National School Brass Band Association   2 Gray's Close, Barton-le-Clay, Bedford MK45 3PH.

Orff-Schulwerk Society   31 Roedean Crescent, London SW15.

Performing Right Society Ltd   29–33 Berners St, London W1P 4AA.

Pipers' Guild   11 Lambourn Way, Tunbridge Wells, Kent TN12 5AJ.

Pro Corda (National Association for Young String Players)   Silver Birches, Crossfield Place, Weybridge, Surrey KT13 0RG.

Royal Musical Association   Secretary, British Museum, Great Russell St, London WC1B 3DG.

Royal Society of Musicians of Gt Britain   10 Stratford Place, London W1N 9AE.

Rural Music Schools' Association   Little Benslow Hills, Hitchin, Herts SG4 9RD.

Royal School of Church Music   Addington Place, Croydon CR9 5AD.

Schools' Council (Music Committee)   160 Gt Portland Street, London W1.

Schools' Music Association   Jack's Park, Upper Gordon Rd, Camberley, Surrey.

Sing for Pleasure   26 Bedford Square, London WC1B 3H.

Society for Research in the Psychology of Music and Music Education   c/o Dr R. Shuter-Dyson, 19 Hansler Grove, East Molesey, Surrey KT8 9JN.

Society for the Promotion of New Music   29 Exhibition Rd, London SW7 2AS.

Society of Recorder Players   5 Pembroke Avenue, Kenton, Harrow, Middlesex HA3 8QG.

Standing Conference for Amateur Music   26 Bedford Square, London WC1B 3HU.

Tonic Sol-Fa College of Music   18 Holwood Road, Bromley, Kent BR1 3EB.

United Kingdom Council for Music Education   c/o Eric Stapleton, Education Office, Threadneedle House, Market Rd, Chelmsford, Essex CM1 1LD.

Workers' Music Association   236 Westbourne Park Rd, London W11 1EL.

Youth and Music   40 William IV Street, London WC2.

4   Selected course centres

British Federation of Music Festivals (incorporating the Music Teachers' Association)   Summer Schools, 106 Gloucester Place, London W1H 3DB.

Cambridge Ward Method Centre   Newnham College, Cambridge.

Canford Summer School of Music   250 Purley Way, Croydon CR9 4QD.

Children's Concert Centre   Regent Street, Haslingden, Rossendale, Lancs.

Colour Music Studio   Triad Arts Centre, Bishop's Stortford, Herts.

Dalcroze Society   89 Highfield Avenue, London NW11 2RB.

Dartington Hall   Totnes, Devon.

Dolmetsch Summer School   Marley Copse, Marley Common, Haslemere, Surrey.

Ernest Read Music Association (ERMA)   143 King Henry's Road, London NW3 3RD.

International Musicians' Seminar (Advanced Courses)   Prussia, Cove, Cornwall c/o H. Behrens, 11 Park Vista, London SE10.

International Summer School (Advanced Courses)   4 Abbots Barton Walk, Canterbury, Kent CT1 3AY.

Musical Youth International (Music Workshops for Children)   1481 Stratford Rd, Birmingham B28 9HT.

New Music in Action   York Summer School Registrar, Universal Edition, 2/3 Fareham St, London W1V 4DU.

Recorder in Education Summer School   2 Meadowhead Close, Sheffield S8 7TX.

Rural Music Schools' Association   Little Benslow Hills, Hitchin, Herts.

Schools' Music Association   Jack's Park, Upper Gordon Road, Camberley, Surrey.

Sing for Pleasure Summer School   26 Bedford Square, London WC1N 3HU.

Snape Maltings Foundation (Advanced Courses)   Education Administrator, Festival Office, High Street, Aldeburgh, Suffolk 1P 15 5AY.

Stowe Summer School of Music   Willowdown, Megg Lane, Chipperfield, Herts WD4 9JN.

Wavendon All-Music Plan (WAP)   The Stables, Wavendon, Milton Keynes MK17 8LT.

5   Selected instrument makers and/or distributors

Arnold, E. J.   Butterley Street, Leeds LS10 1AX

Boosey & Hawkes (Musical Instruments) Ltd   Deansbrook Road, Edgware, Middlesex HA8 9BB.

Buffet-Crampton   Pages Walk, London SE1.

Dolmetsch, A. Ltd   Kings Road, Haslemere, Surrey GU27 2QJ.

Foote, Chas. E. Ltd   17 Golden Square, London W1.

Hohner, H. Ltd   39/45 Coldharbour Lane, London SE5 9NR.

Rose-Morris & Co Ltd   32–34 Gordon House Road, London NW5 1NE.

Rosetti   The House of Music, 138–140 Old Street, London EC1V 9BL.

Schott   48 Great Marlborough Street, London W1V 2BN.

6   Selected music publishers

(A source of catalogues; inspection service; parts on rental for large-scale works; advice)

Arnold, E. J. & Sons   Lockwood, Parkside Lane, Leeds LS1 5TD.

Ashdown, Edwin   275–281 Cricklewood, Broadway, London NW2 6QR (Specializes in easy piano music)

Associated Board of the Royal Schools of Music   14 Bedford Square, London WC1B 3JG.

Banks Music Publications   139 Holgate Road, York YO2 4DF.

Belwin-Mills Music Ltd   230 Purley Way, Croydon CR9 4QD.

Boosey & Hawkes Ltd   295 Regent Street, London W1R 8JH.

Bosworth & Co. Ltd   14–18 Heddon Street, Regent Street, London W1R 8DP.

Breitkopf & Härtel (London) Ltd   8 Horse and Dolphin Yard, Macclesfield Street, London W1V 7LG.

Brons Music Service   64 Dean Street, London W1V 5HG (specializes in brass band and light music)

Cambridge University Press   Bentley House, 200 Euston Road, London NW1 2DB

Chappell & Co. Ltd   50 New Bond Street, London W1A 2BR.

Cramer & Co. Ltd   99 St. Martin's Lane, London WC2N 4AZ.

Emerson Edition   Windmill Farm, Ampleforth, Yorkshire (specializing in wind music).

Faber Music Ltd   38 Russell Square, London WC1B 5DA.

Forsyth   126 Deansgate, Manchester M3 2GR.

Hinrichsen Edition Ltd & Peters Edition   10–12 Baches Street, London N1 6DN.

Middle Eight Music Ltd   7 Garrick Street, London WC2E 9AR (specializing in popular & light music for educational use)

Novello & Co. Ltd   1–3 Upper James Street, London W1R 4BP.

Oxford University Press Music Department   44 Conduit Street, London W1.

Piper Publications   Ash House, Yarnfield, Stone, Staffs. (ensemble & orchestral music)

Regina Music Publishing Co. Ltd   Old Run Road, Leeds LS10 2AA (specializing in music for young children).

Roberton Publications   The Windmill, Wendover, Aylesbury, Bucks HP22 6JJ.

Royal School of Church Music   Addington Palace, Croydon, CR9 5AD. (for church music and training booklets)

Schott & Co. Ltd   48 Gt Marlborough Street, London W1V 2BN (published Orff-Schulwerk).

Stainer & Bell Ltd   82 High Road, East Finchley, London N2 9PW.

Universal Edition   2/3 Fareham Street, Dean Street, London W1V 4DU.

Weinberger, J. Ltd   10–16 Rathbone Street, London W1P 2BJ (specializes in dramatic works).

7   Local contacts

For information on private tuition one can contact

1   The Citizen's Advice Bureau or Civic Information Centre who should be able to supply contacts and the secretary's address of the local branch of the Incorporated Society of Musicians

2   Area Music Adviser
A list of advisers covering the United Kingdom can be obtained from
Muriel Blackwell
Musical Adviser
London Borough of Brent
Educational Department
PO Box 1, Chesterfield House
9 Park Lane
Wembley, Middlesex

3   The Local Music Shop
Most music shops keep a register of private teachers.

4   In addition to the above sources of information the Yellow Pages of the Telephone Directory and the Classified Columns of the local newspaper contain advertisements for music teachers, musical instrument and music shops, repairers and tuners etc.

For information on classes (including evening classes), band and orchestra membership consult

1   your local library
2   the local education area officer
3   area music adviser
4   local adult education centre
5   nearest Workers' Educational Association Branch, university, college, polytechnic

References and Bibliography

ADAMS, D. J. (1970) 'Music and the deaf', *Music in Education*, Vol. 34, no. 345, Sept./Oct, London: Novello.

ADAMS, S. (1968) 'The development of instrumental music', *Music Teacher*, Vol. 47, nos 2 and 3, Feb./March, London: Evans Brothers.

AICKEN, F. (1975) 'Fanning the fires of imagination', *Times Educational Supplement*, July 4th, 1975.

ALDERSON, M. F. and COLLES, H. C. (1943) *History of St Michael's College, Tenbury*, London: SPCK.

ALVIN, J. (1966) *Music Therapy*, London: John Baker.

ANNAN (1975) 'The university in Britain', *Universities for a Changing World*, M. D. Stephens and G. W. Roderick (eds) Newton Abbot: David & Charles.

ASHTON, B. (1975) 'Music and all that jazz', *Times Educational Supplement*, June 13th, 1975.

ATTWOOD, T. (1975) 'Pop music as a CSE option', *Music Teacher*, Vol. 54, no. 11, November.

ATTWOOD, T. (1977) *Bibliography of Pop Music in Education*, London: Cockpit Arts Workshop (mimeo).

ATTWOOD, T. & FARMER, P. (1977) *Pop Workbook*, London: Edward Arnold.

BAILEY, K. V. (1974) 'Future developments: a note', *Trends in Education*, no. 36, December, London: HMSO.

BAILEY, P. (1973) *They Can Make Music*, London: Oxford University Press.

BARCLAY, W. (1959) *Educational Ideals in the Ancient World*, London: Collins.

BARNES, K. (1973) *Twenty Years of Pop*, London: Kenneth Mason.

BARTLETT, I. (1976) 'An historical view of tonic sol-fa', *Music Teacher*, Vol. 55, no. 5, May.

BBC (1966) *Educational Television and Radio in Britain*, London: BBC.

BBC (1974) *After Fifty Years the Future*, London: BBC.

BENTLEY, A. (1953) 'The training of specialist teachers of music in the university of Reading', *Music in Education*, UNESCO (ed) Paris: Unesco.

BENTLEY, A. (1966) *Musical Ability in Children and its Measurement*, London: Harrap & Co.

BENTLEY, A. (1975) *Music in Education: a point of view*, Slough: National Foundation for Educational Research.

BERGMANN, W. (1969) 'A bird's eye view of recorder music', *Music Teacher*, Vol. 48, no. 5, May.

BITCON, C. (1969) 'Orff-Schulwerk': clinical application (mimeo).

BLAIR, D. (1970) Chairman's Address, *British Journal of Music Therapy* Vol. 2, no. 1.

BLOOM, B. S. (1956) *Taxonomy of Educational Objectives Handbook 1: cognitive domain, Handbook 2: affective domain* (pub. 1964), London: Longmans.

BOARD OF EDUCATION (1926) *The Education of the Adolescent* (the Hadow Report) London: HMSO.

BOARD OF EDUCATION (1933) *Recent Developments in School Music*, Pamphlet 95, London: HMSO.

BOARD OF EDUCATION (1938) *Report of the Consultative Committee on*

Secondary Education with Special Reference to Grammar Schools and Technical High Schools (the Spens Report) London: HMSO.

BONHAM-CARTER, V. (1958) *Dartington Hall: the history of an experiment*, London: Phoenix House.

BONTINCK, I. (ed.) (1974) *New Patterns of Musical Behaviour*, London: Universal.

BRACE, G. (1970) *Music in the Secondary School Timetable*, University of Exeter: Institute of Education.

BRAMWELL, R. D. (1961) *Elementary School Work 1900–1925*, University of Durham, Institute of Education.

BRAUN, E. B. (1973) *Montessori and Music: rhythmic activities for young children*, New York: Schocker.

BROCKLEHURST, B. (1971) *Response to Music*, London: Routledge and Kegan Paul.

BRUCE, V. R. (1970) *Movement in Silence and Sound*, London: G. Bell & Sons.

BRUCE, V. R. (1972) 'Hinder not music', *Music Teacher*, Vol. 51, no. 8, August.

BURNETT, M. (1972) 'Coming to terms with pop', *Music Teacher*, Vol. 51, nos 2–11, February to November.

BURNETT, M. (1977) *Music Education Review*, Volume 1, London: Chappell & Co.

BURNS, W. (1968) 'Report of conference on leisure', *The Guardian*, September 10th, 1968.

BUTTERWORTH, A. (1970) 'The brass band: a cloth cap joke', *Music in Education*, Vol. 34, no. 342, 343 March/April, May/June.

CAMBRIDGESHIRE REPORT (1933) *Music and the Community*, London: Cambridge University Press.

CAMPBELL, L. (1976) 'Whatever happened to Dalcroze Eurhythmics', *Music Teacher*, Vol. 55, No. 6, June.

CARLTON, M. (1978) 'Repertory: Wind Band Music in Education', *Music in Education*, Vol. 42, No. 391, March.

CENTRAL ADVISORY COUNCIL FOR EDUCATION (1963) *Half Our Future* (the Newsom Report) London: HMSO.

CHARLTON, P. (1971–2) *The Development of Musical Appreciation in Secondary Schools in England 1900–1950*, unpublished MEd thesis University of Leicester.

CHOKSY, L. (1974) *The Kodály Method: comprehensive music education from infant to adult*, Englewood Cliffs, New Jersey: Prentice-Hall.

CLEMENTS, J. (1974) 'Bring us back to doh', *Times Educational Supplement*, November 1st, 1974.

COHEN, L. (1976) *Educational Research in Classrooms and Schools: a manual of materials and methods*, London: Harper and Row.

COLE, H. (1972) 'Suzuki talent education', *Music in Education*, Vol. 36, no. 356, July/August.

COOKE, D. (1959) *The Language of Music*, London: Oxford University Press.

COOPER, C. (1976) 'Using colour', *Music Teacher*, Vol. 55, no. 7, July.

COOPER, R. (1974) 'In search of the unthinkable', *Times Educational Supplement*, 1 February 1974.

COUNCIL OF EUROPE (1976) *Towards Cultural Democracy*, Strasbourg: Council of Europe.

COUNCIL OF EUROPE (1976) *Cultural Policy in Towns*, Strasbourg: Council of Europe.

CRANMER, P. (1975) 'Examining far and wide', *Times Educational Supplement*, 7 February 1975.

CRUMP, P. (1978) 'In the steps of Suzuki', *Times Educational Supplement*, 21 April.

CURWEN, J. (1843) *Singing for Schools in Congregations: a course of instructing a School*, London.

CURWEN, J. (1858) *Standard Course of Tonic Sol-Fa*, London: Curwen.

DALCROZE, E. J. (1921) *Rhythm, Music and Education*, Pyrford: Dalcroze Society.

DAVIES, J. B. (1978) *The Psychology of Music*, London: Hutchinson.

DAVIES, P. M. (1963) 'Music', *The Arts and Current Tendencies in Education* Studies in Education (ed. University of London Institute of Education) London: Evans Brothers.

DENT, H. C. (1961) *Universities in Transition*, London: Cohen and West.

DEPARTMENT OF EDUCATION AND SCIENCE (1967) *Statistics in Education*, 1965, London: HMSO.

DEPARTMENT OF EDUCATION AND SCIENCE (1972a) *Education: a framework for expansion*, Parliamentary White Paper, London: HMSO.

DEPARTMENT OF EDUCATION AND SCIENCE (1972b) *Movement: physical education in the primary years*, London: HMSO.

DEPARTMENT OF EDUCATION AND SCIENCE (1972c) *Teacher Education and Training: report of the committee of inquiry into the education and training of teachers* (the James Report) London: HMSO.

DEPARTMENT OF EDUCATION AND SCIENCE (1973) *Adult Education: a plan for development* (the Russell Report), London: HMSO.

DEPARTMENT OF EDUCATION AND SCIENCE (1975) *Statistics in Education 1973, Vol. 2: School Leavers, CSE and GCE* and *Vol. 6 Universities*, London: HMSO.

DEPARTMENT OF EDUCATION AND SCIENCE (1977) *Gifted Children in Middle and Comprehensive Schools*, HMI Series: matters for discussion, London: HMSO.

DEPARTMENT OF EDUCATION AND SCIENCE (1978) *Discussion Document: higher education into the 1990s*, London: HMSO.

DEPARTMENT OF EDUCATION AND SCIENCE (1978) *Report of the Working Group on the Management of Higher Education in the Maintained Sector* (the Oakes Report), London: HMSO.

DEPARTMENT OF EDUCATION AND SCIENCE (1978) *Special Educational Needs: report of the committee of enquiry into the education of handicapped children and young people* (the Warnock Report), London: HMSO.

DEWEY, J. (1934) *Art as Experience*, New York: Minton, Balch & Co.

DICKINSON, P. I. (1976) *Music with ESN Children*, Slough: National Federation for Educational Research.

DIGGLE, K. (1975) 'Sponsorship of the arts', *The Guardian*, 23 October.

DOBBS, J. P. B. (1964) *Three Pioneers of Sight-Singing in the Nineteenth Century*, Institutes of Education of Durham and Newcastle.

DOBBS, J. P. B. (1966) *The Slow Learner and Music*, London: Oxford University Press.

DOBBS, J. P. B. (1975) '50 years of music at Dartington', *Music in Education*, Vol. 39, no. 376, November/December.

DOMAN, G. (1965) *Teach Your Baby to Read*, London: Jonathan Cape.

DONINGTON, R. (1932) *The Work and Ideas of Arnold Dolmetsch*, Haslemere; Dolmetsch Foundation.

DOUGLAS, A. (1968) *The Electronic Musical Instrument Manual*, London: Pitman Publishing.

DOUGLAS, A. (1973) *Electronic Music Production*, London: Pitman Publishing.

DRIVER, E. (1951) *Pathway to Dalcroze Eurhythmics*, London: Nelson.

DUTOIT, C. (1971) *Music, Movement, Therapy*, Pyrford: Dalcroze Society.

EAST, J. M. (1978) The MIE guide to adult music education in London, *Music in Education*, Vol. 42, no. 395, July.

EDUCATION GUARDIAN (1976) 'Moving up the examination charts', *The Guardian*, 8 June 1976.

ERIKSON, E. (1950) *Childhood and Society*, New York: W. W. Norton & Co.

FARMER, P. (1976) 'Pop music in the secondary school: a justification', *Music in Education*, Vol. 40, no. 381, September/October.

FARMER, P. (1977) 'Examining Pop', *Music in Education*, Vol. 41, no. 387, September/October.

FAWDRY, K. (1974) *Everything but Alf Garnett: a personal view of BBC school broadcasting*, London: BBC.

FORBES, P. (undated) *Report on Separated GCE Music Syllabus* (mimeo).

FOSTER, J. (1977) *The Influence of Rudolf Laban*, London: Lepus Books.

GARSON, A. (1971) 'The Suzuki teaching method', *Music in Education*, Vol. 35, no. 348, March/April.

GILBERT, J. (1975) *Musical Activities with Young Children*, London: Ward Lock.

GLOVER, S. (1835) *Scheme for Rendering Psalmody Congregational; comprising a key to the sol-fa notation of music and directions for instructing a school*, London.

GOLDING, P. (1974) *The Mass Media*, London: Longman.

GOODRIDGE, J. (1970) *Drama in the Primary School*, London: Heinemann Educational Books Ltd.

GRAY, V. and PERCIVAL, R. (1962) *Music, Movement and Mime for Children*, London: Oxford University Press.

GRIFFITHS, P. (1977) 'The York project', *Music in Education*, Vol. 41, no. 384, March/April.

GULBENKIAN (1965) *Making Musicians: a report to the Calouste Gulbenkian Foundation*, London: Calouste Gulbenkian Foundation.

GULBENKIAN (1978) *Training Musicians: a report to the Calouste Gulbenkian Foundation on the training of professional musicians*, London: Calouste Gulbenkian Foundation.

HALL, S. and WHANNEL, P. (1964) *The Popular Arts*, London: Hutchinson Educational.

HALE, N. V. (1947) *Education for Music: a skeleton plan of research into the development of the study of music as part of the organized plan of general education*. London: Oxford University Press.

HART, M. (1974) *Music*, London: Heinemann Educational.

HATCH, T. (1976) *So You Want to be in the Music Business*, London: Everest Books.

HAYTER, C. G. (1974) *The Use of Broadcasts in Schools: a survey and evaluation*, London: BBC/ITV Publications.

HERMANN, E. J. (1965) *Supervising Music in the Elementary School*, Englewood Cliffs, New Jersey: Prentice-Hall.

HEWETT, S. (1975) 'Foreword', *Summary of Courses at Colleges and Departments of Education* (ed. Association of Teachers in Colleges and Departments of Education) London: Lund Humphries.

HIGGINS, A. P. (1966) *Talking About Television*, London: British Film Institute.

HIMMELWEIT, H., OPPENHEIM, A. H. and VINCE, P. (1958) *Television and the Child*, London: Oxford University Press.

HOFFER, C. R. (1974) 'Youth, music education and the new sound environment', *New Patterns of Musical Behaviour* Bontinck, I. (ed.) London: Universal.

HORTON, J. (1969) 'Some great music educators 10: Carl Orff', *Music Teacher*, Vol. 48, nos. 4 and 5, April May.

HOZIER, J. (1963) 'Television joins sound in BBC primary broadcasting', *Music in Education*, Vol. 27, no. 300, March/April.

HUBICKI, M. (1972) 'The philosophy behind colour staff', *Music in Education*, Vol. 36, no. 356, July/August.

HUNT, A. (1976) *Listen: Lets Make Music*, London: Bedford Square Press.

IBBERSON, M. (1978) *For Joy that We are Here*, London: Bedford Square Press.

JACOBS, A. (ed.) (1976) *Music Education Handbook*, London and New York: Bowker.

JASPER, T. (1975) *Simply Pop*, London: Queen Anne Press.

JOHN, M. (1971) *Music Drama in Schools*, London: Cambridge University Press.

JOHNSON, R. W. (1968) 'Music in a liberal education — the role of GCE examinations in the school music curriculum', *Music in Education*, Vol. 32, no. 330, March/April.

JONES, C. (1975) 'Incest or Incentive', *Visual Education*, October, London: National Committee for Audio Visual Aids in Education.

JOR, F. (1976) *The Demystification of Culture*, Strasbourg: Council of Europe.

KAHN, N. (1976) *The Arts Britain Ignores*, London: Community Relations Council, Calouste Gulbenkian Foundation, Arts Council.

KAROLYI, O. (1965) *Introducing Music*, Harmondsworth: Penguin.

KARPELES, M. (1967) *Cecil Sharp, his Life and Work*, London: Routledge & Kegan Paul.

KEETMAN, G. (1974) *Elementaria: first acquaintance with Orff-Schulwerk*, M. Murray (trans.) London: Schott & Co.

KENDELL, I. (1974) *Music Education of Young Children: a general introduction to the trial materials*, University of Reading/Schools Council Research and Development Project (mimeo).

KENDELL, I. (1975) 'Primary project's new phase', *Times Educational Supplement*, 7 February.

KENNARD, D. J. (1978) *Access to Music for the Physically Handicapped Schoolchild and School Leaver*, London: Disabled Living Foundation.

KRAUS, E. (ed.) (1978) *ISME Yearbook Vol. 4: The Education of Professional Musicians*, London: Schott.

LANGER, S. K. (1967) *Mind: an essay on human feeling*, Baltimore: Johns Hopkins Press.

LAWRENCE, I. (1975) *Music and the Teacher*, London: Pitman Publishing.

LEONARD, C. and HOUSE, R. W. (1959) *Foundations and Principles of Music Education*, (rev. 1972) New York: McGraw Hill.

LIVINGS, H. (1975) *That the Medals and the Baton be put on View: the story of a village band 1875–1975*, Newton Abbot: David & Charles.

LOFTHOUSE, P. (1970) *Dance*, London: Heinemann Educational.

LONG, N. (1959) *Music in English Education*, London: Faber.

LOWERY, H. (1963) 'Music and liberal studies or challenges in musical education' *Music in Education: proceedings of the 14th symposium of the colston research society*, London: Butterworth.

LUNDIN, R. W. (1953) *An Objective Psychology of Music*, New York: Ronald Press Co.

MCCALDIN, D. (1968) 'Music in a liberal education forum No. 2; the universities', *Music in Education*, Vol. 32, no. 333, September/October.

MCLELLAN, J. (1970) *The Question of Play*, Oxford: Pergamon Press.

MACONIE, R. (1975a) 'All together now', *Times Educational Supplement*, 25 April 1975.

MACONIE, R. (1975b) 'Metamorphosis in taste', *Times Educational Supplement*, 11 July 1975.

MACPHERSON, S. and READ, E. (1912) *Aural Culture Based Upon Musical Appreciation*, London: Joseph Williams.

MACPHERSON, S. (1923) *The Appreciation Class*, London: Joseph Williams.

MADSEN, C. K., GREEN, R. D. and MADSEN, C. H. (eds.) (1975) *Research in Music Behaviour: modifying music behaviour in the classroom*, New York: Teachers' College Press.

MAINZER, J. (1841/2) *The National Singing Circular*, London.

MAINZER, J. (1841/2) *Singing for the Million: a practical course of musical instruction in two parts*, London.

MARAIS, E. M. (1965) 'Adventures in music with subnormal children', *Music in Education*, Vol. 29, no. 315, September/October.

MARSHALL, J. (1972) 'Pop go the telly tunes', *The Guardian*, 7 June.

MARSHALL, S. (1963) *An Experiment in Education*, London: Cambridge University Press.

MARSHALL, S. (1968) *Adventure in Creative Education*, Oxford: Pergamon.

MEE, E. C. (1974) 'Fifty years of school broadcasting and the changing curricula of primary schools 1924–74', *Trends in Education*, no. 36, December, London: HMSO.

MEYER-DENKMANN, G. (1977) *Experiments in Sound*, London: Universal.

MILLS, E. and MURPHY, ST. T. C. (eds.) (1974) *The Suzuki Concept*, New York: Diablo Press.

MINIHAN, J. (1977) *The Nationalization of Culture: the development of state subsidies for the arts in Great Britain*, London: Hamish Hamilton.

MINISTRY OF EDUCATION (1952) *Schools Broadcasts: a sample study from the listeners' end*, Pamphlet no. 20. London: HMSO.

MINISTRY OF EDUCATION (1959) *15 to 18: report of the Central Advisory Council for Education – England* (The Crowther Report), London: HMSO.

MINISTRY OF EDUCATION (1967) *Children and their Primary Schools* (The Plowden Report), London: HMSO.

MOOG, H. (1976) *The Musical Experience of the Pre-School Child*, (trans. C. Clarke) London: Schott.

MOORE, S. S. (1949) *The Golden String*, London: Nelson.

MORE, T. (1968) 'Justine Ward', *Music Teacher*, Vol. 47, no. 12; vol. 48, no. 1, December/January.

MOUTRIE, J. (1968) 'The appreciation movement in Britain: Macpherson, Read and Scholes', *Music Teacher*, Vol. 47, no. 10.

MULHOLLAND, R. (1976) 'Youth music', *Music Teacher*, Vol. 55, nos. 1–4, January–April.

MURSELL, J. L. (1937) *The Psychology of Music*, New York: W. W. Norton & Co.

MURSELL, J. L. (1948) *Education for Musical Growth*, Boston: Ginn.

MYER, M. G. (1974) 'Feeding the tradition', *Times Educational Supplement* 9 August.

NETTEL, R. (1952) *The Englishman Makes Music (Account of Music in Social Life in this Country during 18th and 19th Centuries)*, London: Dennis Dobson.

NORDOFF, P. and ROBBINS, C. (1971) *Therapy in Music for Handicapped Children*, London: Gollancz.

NORDOFF, P. and ROBBINS, C. (1975 *Music Therapy in Special Education*, London: MacDonald and Evans.

ORGANIZATION FOR ECONOMIC CO-OPERATION AND DEVELOPMENT (1977) *Education Policies and Trends*, Paris: OECD.

ORFF, C. (1964) 'Orff-Schulwerk: past and future', *Music in Education*, Vol. 28, no. 309, September/October.

ORFF, C. and KEETMAN, G. (1958) *Orff-Schulwerk Music for Children*, M. Murray (trans.) London: Schott & Co.

PALMER, T. (1970) *Born under a Bad Sign*, London: William Kimber.

PAPE, M. (1970) *Growing Up With Music*, London: Oxford University Press.

PARKER, S. (1976) *The Sociology of Leisure*, London: George Allen and Unwin.

PAYNTER, J. and ASTON, P. (1970) *Sound and Silence: classroom projects in creative music*, London: Cambridge University Press.

PAYNTER, J. (1972) *Hear and Now*, London: Universal.

PAYNTER, J. (1973) 'Still lagging behind', *Times Educational Supplement*, 16 February.

PICKERING, W. (1968) 'Religion – a leisure time pursuit?', *A Sociological Yearbook of Religion*, D. Martin, (ed.) London: SCM Press.

RAINBOW, B. (ed.) (1964) *Handbook for Music Teachers*, (rev. 1968) London: Novello & Co.

RAINBOW, B. (1967) *The Land Without Music*, London: Novello & Co.

READ, H. (1958) *Education Through Art*, London: Faber.

REDCLIFFE-MAUD (1976) *Support for the Arts in England and Wales*, London: Calouste Gulbenkian Foundation.

REGELSKI, T. (1975) *Principles and Problems of Music Education*, Englewood Cliffs, New Jersey: Prentice-Hall.

RENOUF, D. (1960) *The Teaching of Music in English Schools: historical background and contemporary trends* unpublished M.A. thesis Institute of Education, University of London.

ROSS, M. (1975) *Arts and the Adolescent*, Schools Council Working Paper 54, London: Evans/Methuen Educational.

RURAL MUSIC SCHOOLS ASSOCIATION (1977) *The Suzuki Investigation in Hertfordshire*, London: Bedford Square Press.

RUSSELL-SMITH, G. (1969) 'Zoltan Kodály: composer, musicologist and educational revolutionary', *Music Teacher*, Vol. 48, nos 2 and 3, February and March.

RUSSELL-SMITH, G. (1977) *Be a Real Musician*, London: Boosey & Hawkes.

RUSSELL-SMITH, G. (1978) *Be a Better Musician*, London: Boosey & Hawkes.

SÁNDOR, F. (ed.) (1966) *Musical Education in Hungary*, London: Barrie and Rockliffe.

SANTS, J. and BUTCHER, H. J. (eds.) (1975) *Developmental Psychology*, Harmondsworth: Penguin.

SAUNDERS, G. (1978) 'Which recorder', *Music in Education*, Vol. 42, no. 391, March.

SCHAFER, R. M. (1965) *The Composer in the Classroom*, London: Universal.

SCHAFER, R. M. (1967) *Ear Cleaning*, London: Universal.

SCHAFER, R. M. (1973) 'Sound, environment, communication', *Cultures: music and society*, Vol. 1, no. 1, Paris: Unesco et la Baconnière.

SCHAFER, R. M. (1975) *The Rhinoceros in the Classroom*, London: Universal.

SCHNEIDER, U. V. (1964) *Music and Medicine*, Johannesburg: Witwatersrand University Press.

SCHOLES, P. (1947) *The Mirror of Music: Vols I and II*, London: Novello.

SCHOOLS COUNCIL (1966) *The Certificate of Secondary Education: experimental examinations 'Music'*, Examinations Bulletin no. 10.

SCHOOLS COUNCIL (1968a) *Enquiry 1: young school leavers*, London: HMSO.

SCHOOLS COUNCIL (1968b) *The First Three Years 1964/7*, London: HMSO.

SCHOOLS COUNCIL (1971) *Music and the Young School Leaver; problems and opportunities*, Schools Council Working Paper 35, London: Evans/Methuen Educational.

SCHOOLS COUNCIL MUSIC COMMITTEE (1972) *Music and Integrated Studies in the Secondary School*, Autumn Bulletin, London: HMSO.

SCHOOLS MUSIC ASSOCIATION (1962) *Music in Primary Schools*, London: Schools' Music Association.

SEASHORE, C. (1919) *The Psychology of Musical Talent*, New York: Silver, Burdett & Co.

SELF, G. (1965) 'Contemporary music in the classroom', *Music in Education*, Vol. 29, no. 315, September/October.

SERGEANT, D. (1969) 'Experimental investigation of absolute pitch', *Journal of Research in Music Education*, XVII, no. 1, Spring, Washington: MENC.

SHEPHERD, J., VIRDEN, P., VULLIAMY, G. and WISHART, T. (1978) *Whose Music? a sociology of musical languages*, London: Latimer.

SHARP, C. and BARING-GOULD, S. (1906) *English Folk Songs for Schools*, London: Curwen.

SHUTER, R. (1966) 'Hereditary and environmental factors in musical ability', *The Eugenics Review*, no. 58, September.

SHUTER, R. (1968) *The Psychology of Musical Ability*, London: Methuen.

SIMPSON, K. (1963) 'The professional training of music teachers in England and Wales', *Music in Education Proceedings of the 14th Symposium of the Colston Research Society*, London: Butterworth.

SIMPSON, K. (1969) 'Some great music educators 11: conclusion part 1: some questions', *Music Teacher*, Vol. 48, no. 6, June.

SIMPSON, K. (ed.) (1976) *Some Great Music Educators*, London: Novello.

SLADE, P. (1954) *Child Drama*, London: University of London Press.

SLADE, P. (1968) *Experience of Spontaneity*, London: Longmans Green & Co.

SMALL, C. (1978) *Music – Society – Education*, London: John Calder.

STANDING CONFERENCE FOR AMATEUR MUSIC (1966) *Music Centres and the Training of Specially Talented Children*, London: Bedford Square Press.

STANDING CONFERENCE OF MUSIC COMMITTEES (1954) *The Training of Music Teachers*, London: Bedford Square Press.

STANFORD, SIR C. V. (1906) *The National Song Book*, London: Boosey & Co.

SUZUKI, S. (1969) *Nurtured by Love: a new approach to education*, Jericho, New York: Exposition Press.

SWANWICK, K. (1968) *Popular Music and the Teacher*, Oxford: Pergamon Press.

SWANWICK, K. (1972) 'The audio-visual stave', *Music Teacher*, Vol. 51, no. 9, September.

SZÖNYI, E. (1973) *Kodály's Principles in Practice*, Budapest: Corvina Press.

SZÖNYI, E. (1974) *Musical Reading and Writing*, Books 1 and 2, London: Boosey & Hawkes.

TAYLOR, D. (1975) 'Kodály Course', *Music Teacher*, Vol. 54, no. 11, November.

TAYLOR, D. (1977) *Trends and Factors in the Teaching of School Music in Britain with Particular Reference to the 1965–75 Decade*, MA thesis, University of Sheffield.

TAYLOR, R. (1973) 'First in the field', *Music in Education*, Vol. 37, no. 360, March/April.

THACKRAY, R. (1972) *Rhythmic Abilities in Children*, Music Education Research Papers no. 5, London: Novello & Co.

THOMSON, W. (1971) *Introduction to Music as Structure*, Reading, Mass.: Addison-Wesley.

TUCKER, N. (1966) *Understanding the Mass Media*, London: Cambridge University Press.

TYE, R. and TYE, V. (1957) *Music in the Elementary School*, (rev. 1977) Englewood Cliffs, New Jersey: Prentice-Hall.

UNESCO (1953) *Music in Education*, Paris: UNESCO.

UNESCO (1977) *Thinking Ahead – Unesco and the Challenge of Today and Tomorrow*, Paris: UNESCO.

UNIVERSITIES COUNCIL FOR ADULT EDUCATION (1970) *University Adult Education in the Later Twentieth Century*, London: Universities Council for Adult Education.

UNIVERSITY CENTRAL COUNCIL FOR ADMISSIONS (1976) *Fourteenth Report 1975–76*, London: UCCA.

VAJDA, C. (1974) *The Kodály Way to Music*, London: Boosey & Hawkes.

VALENTINE, C. W. (1938) *Examinations and the Examinee*, Birmingham: Birmingham Printers Ltd.

VAN DER EYKEN, W. and TURNER, B. (1969) *Adventures in Education*, Harmondsworth: Penguin.

VULLIAMY, G. and LEE, E. (eds.) (1976) *Pop Music in School*, London: Cambridge University Press.

WALKER, D. (1976) 'Universities defend academic challenge of 'O' levels', *Times Higher Educational Supplement*, 9 April.

WARD, D. (1973) *Singing in Special Schools*, London: Bedford Square Press.

WARD, D. (1976) *Hearts and Hands and Voices*, London: Oxford University.

WESTRUP, J. H. (1967) *An Introduction to Musical History*, London: Hutchinson.

WHITCOMB, I. (1972) *After the Ball*, Harmondsworth: Penguin.

WHITE, E. W. (1975) *The Arts Council of Great Britain*, London: Davis-Poynter.

WILES, J. and GARRARD, G. A. (1957) *Leap to Life*, (rev. 1970) London: Chatto & Windus.

WILLSON, R. B. (1977) *Musical Merry-Go-Round: musical activities for the very young*, London: Heinemann.

WING, H. D. (1948) 'Tests of musical ability and appreciation', *British Journal of Psychology Monogram Supplement No. 27*, London: Cambridge University Press.

WINN, C. (1954) *Teaching Music*, London: Oxford University Press.

WISBEY, A. (1977) 'Music towards reading', *Music in Education*, Vol. 40, no. 386, July/August.

WITKIN, R. W. (1974) *The Intelligence of Feeling*, London: Heinemann Educational.

YOUNG, P. (1964) *Zoltan Kodály: a Hungarian musician*, London: Ernest Benn.